The New
PUZZLE
Classics

Ingenious Twists on Timeless Favorites

OFFICIAL MENSA PUZZLE BOOK

SERHIY GRABARCHUK

Foreword by Will Shortz

Sterling Publishing Co., Inc.
New York

BOOK DESIGN: RENATO STANISIC
ILLUSTRATIONS: SERHIY GRABARCHUK
COPYEDITOR AND PUZZLE CHECKING: ADAM COHEN
EDITOR: RODMAN PILGRIM NEUMANN

Library of Congress Cataloging-in-Publication Data
Grabarchuk, Serhiy.
The new puzzle classics : ingenious twists on timeless favorites / Serhiy Grabarchuk ;
p. cm.
"Official Mensa Puzzle Book."
Includes index.
ISBN 1-4027-1742-3
1. Puzzles. I. Mensa. II. Title.
GV1493.G68 2005
793.73—dc22

2004025979

2 4 6 8 10 9 7 5 3 1

Published by Sterling Publishing Co., Inc.
387 Park Avenue South, New York, NY 10016
© 2005 by Serhiy Grabarchuk
Distributed in Canada by Sterling Publishing
c/o Canadian Manda Group, 165 Dufferin Street
Toronto, Ontario, Canada M6K 3H6
Distributed in Great Britain by Chrysalis Books Group PLC
The Chrysalis Building, Bramley Road, London W10 6SP, England
Distributed in Australia by Capricorn Link (Australia) Pty. Ltd.
P.O. Box 704, Windsor, NSW 2756, Australia

Printed in China
All rights reserved

Sterling ISBN 1-4027-1742-3

For information about custom editions, special sales, premium
and corporate purchases, please contact Sterling Special Sales
Department at 800-805-5489 or specialsales@sterlingpub.com.

The New
PUZZLE
Classics

To Martin Gardner, my Teacher,
who has opened to me thousands of ways
to the Puzzle Universe.

Acknowledgments

The author would like to express his gratitude to the following puzzle folks for their kind support, inspiration, and permission to use their contributions to this book: Martin Gardner, Jerry Slocum, Nob Yoshigahara, Will Shortz, Bill Ritchie, Antoly Kalinin, Vladimir Rybinskiy, Andy Liu, Ed Pegg Jr., Erich Friedman, Nick Baxter, Susan Hoover, Oyvind Tafjord, Jean-Charles Meyrignac, Koji Kitajima, Hiroshi Yamamoto, Setsuo Sasaki, Hirokazu Iwasawa, Tom Hull, Tanya Grabarchuk, Peter Grabarchuk, and Serhiy Grabarchuk Jr. Solutions to the Origami Checkerboard Puzzle were first presented at www.puzzles.com, and are used here with permission of Bill Ritchie of ThinkFun, Inc.

Contents

Foreword by Will Shortz 11

Preface 13

Puzzles 15

1. Puzzling Dissections **16**

2. Dot-Connections **42**

3. Matchsticks & Coins **72**

4. Witty Patterns **98**

5. Words & Numbers **127**

6. Origami Puzzles **154**

7. Tricky Moves **182**

8. Challenging Mix **210**

Solutions 241

Index 346

Foreword

In the world of mathematical and logical puzzles, completely new ideas are rare. Most books of this genre take existing puzzles—generally, the classics, because they're classics for a reason—perhaps modify them a bit, and present them as "new." Sometimes the author throws in a few original creations. And thus does the world's corpus of math and logic puzzles slowly increase.

Serhiy Grabarchuk's work is different. An engineer by training from Uzhgorod, Ukraine, he has been creating strikingly original puzzles for at least twenty-five years. And every one is based on a new idea.

I first learned of Serhiy around 1991 from my friend Scot Morris, the "Games" columnist for the late, lamented *Omni* magazine.

In response to my letter, Serhiy sent me a copy of his first book, self-published in Russian—*Jug with Diamonds: Twelve Oriental Tales and Twelve Puzzles*. As the title indicated, it contained a dozen puzzles, each one mechanical in nature (involving moving pieces), exactingly illustrated by Serhiy himself, and accompanied by a short story. Brief summaries of the puzzle instructions appeared in English, for those of us whose Russian was rusty. Anyone could see at a glance that this was unusual work, and actual solving revealed an astonishingly adept puzzle mind.

With encouragement from puzzle friends and admirers in the West, Serhiy made his first trips abroad to attend events like the International Puzzle Party, an annual gathering of mechanical puzzle inventors and collectors, and the World Puzzle Championship, an annual competition of the world's best solvers.

Soon Serhiy's puzzles were appearing *in* the World Puzzle Championships. Meanwhile, his mechanical puzzles were bought, manufactured, and sold to a growing number of fans by companies such as Bits and Pieces and ThinkFun. Improbably, Serhiy has become one of the few people in the world to earn his living by creating nonword puzzles.

Here at last is Serhiy's first book of puzzles published for a popular, Western audience. I think you'll understand soon what all the excitement is about. It's fresh, varied, and fun.

One more thing: Serhiy has two sons, Serhiy Jr. and Peter, both of whom follow in their father's footsteps and create original puzzles of their own. Their work also shows great elegance and beauty. In fact, who is the greatest puzzle inventor of the Grabarchuk family is still an open question.

———Will Shortz

Preface

One of the most amazing phenomena of mankind is a constant interest in puzzling and puzzles in all of their variety. There are many people who create fun and entertaining—though not always as easy as they seem at first—tasks to challenge other people, who, in turn, love to accept these challenges and solve them.

All puzzles in this book were created as a modern continuation of puzzle traditions formed by greatest puzzle creators of the past, such as Sam Loyd and Henry E. Dudeney. I have done my best not only to create original challenges and to breathe new life into traditional pastimes, but also to find and unfold different perspectives. Many puzzles in this book present totally new ideas, and pose tasks from unexplored fields of the Puzzle Universe.

This book is a collection of modern visual, geometric, word, number, topological, folding, moving, matchstick, coin, and other kinds of puzzles in a wide range of themes and difficulty levels. My aim was to create a book with puzzles ready to solve with pencil or with other simple objects—coins, matches, or toothpicks, square sheets or strips of paper, and similar simple things that always are readily available. I also hope to convey to every reader and solver of this book's puzzles my delight of puzzles and puzzling, and how these incomparable and infinite sources of challenges develop our mind potential, sharpen our wits, train our solving skills, and provide us with clever fun, all in a pleasant and peaceful way.

More than 200 different puzzles included in this book are divided into eight general puzzle categories:

1.—Dissection puzzles

2.—Dot-connection puzzles

3.—Puzzles with matchsticks and coins

4.—Solving pattern puzzles

5.—Puzzles involving words and numbers

6.—Origami puzzles

7.—Puzzles with moving pieces

8.—Other challenging miscellanea

Generally, puzzles of the same kind are gathered into their own, separate chapter. But since the spectrum of puzzles is extremely diverse, puzzles of more general varieties are scattered and interwoven throughout the book. In every chapter easier puzzles are at the beginning, and difficulty increases as the chapter progresses. On the other hand, the visual aspects of puzzles is emphasized, so that within each chapter you will find several groups of similar puzzles also progressing from simple to difficult. Some puzzles provide little hints.

Many challenges in this book are comparable in difficulty to those of the World Puzzle Championship (WPC) and some of them can be hard puzzle nuts to crack. Moreover, several challenges based on the ideas presented in this book were used in previous WPCs and were well received. I believe that every puzzle proposed in this collection can be solved with simple logical reasoning, common sense, clear analysis, some insight, and, above all, a love of puzzles and puzzling. I also hope that, since there is no time limit for solvers—unlike in puzzle competitions—this modern puzzle collection will bring hours of entertaining and intellectual fun for every true puzzle lover—novice and connoisseur alike.

This book is my first big collection gathered in one volume, and I would like to thank Sterling Publishing Co., Inc. for their interest in publishing it. Also I am grateful to my editors at Sterling, Peter Gordon and Rodman Pilgrim Neumann, who skillfully brought the book to its final appearance.

Last but not least, I want to express my deepest gratitude to my wife, Tanya, and my sons, Peter and Serhiy Jr., for their infinite help, understanding, and patience. My kind thanks go to all my friends and puzzle lovers for their constant interest in me and my puzzles, and for providing fantastic feedback. And my very special thanks to every reader of this book. Also, I would be happy and grateful to receive your comments about the book at: serhiy.g@gmail.com. Happy puzzling!

——**Serhiy Grabarchuk**

The New
PUZZLE
Classics

Chapter **1**

PUZZLING DISSECTIONS

Puzzles in this chapter are divided into two groups, which, in fact, represent two of the most popular and traditional types of dissection puzzles—dividing an object into a specified number of pieces, and transforming one shape into other. More dissections are included in several other chapters of this book—puzzles with special dividing that use matchsticks, puzzles with letter- and number-shaped elements, and three-dimensional dissections, among others.

There are some general conditions for solving dissection puzzles, namely:

1. Grids and patterns within (or around) puzzle shapes are provided in order to show the exact proportions of the shapes' elements, and for your convenience. Unless it is specified in the instructions to a particular puzzle, you can use these grids' lines (and patterns depicted on some shapes) as you wish, and you can divide the shapes any way you deem appropriate to solve the puzzle.

2. Every shape's area has to be fully used when you solve the puzzle.

3. Pieces can be rotated as you wish.

4. In puzzles that rearrange one shape(s) into another, no piece can be turned over, and pieces may not overlap.

5. In some puzzles you will be asked to divide a shape into some number of *congruent* pieces. In these cases, pieces must have their outlines be the same—they must coincide exactly when superimposed, no matter how the patterns of their surfaces look. Since congruent pieces may be mirror images of each other, you may have solutions even with some symmetrical pieces disregarding the patterns that their surfaces have.

6. When the instructions of a puzzle ask to get *different* pieces, this means that every possible pair of these pieces must be different at least in their mutual shapes or sizes. Congruent pieces are not to be considered as different.

The Nautilus Puzzle

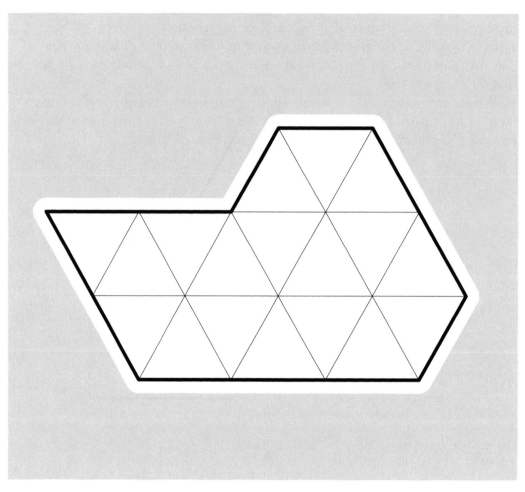

Divide this figure into two *congruent* parts.

The New Puzzle Classics

The Challenge of the Pyramid

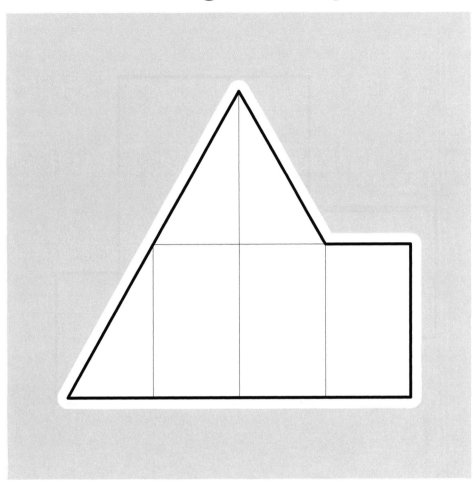

Divide the pyramid into three *congruent* parts.

Triple Cut

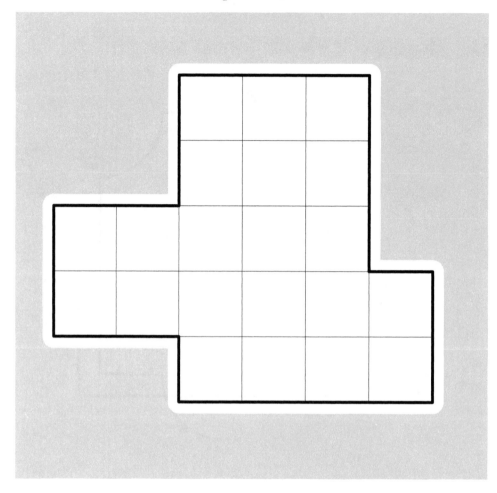

Divide this figure into three *congruent* parts.

The New Puzzle Classics

Cracker Dissection

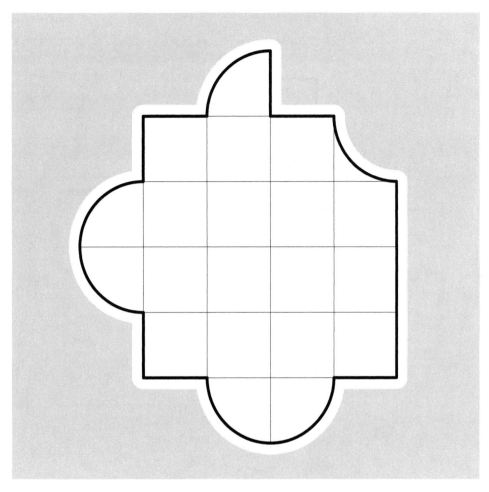

Divide this figure into four *congruent* parts.

Divide the Grid

Divide the wire grid shown above into four *congruent* parts.

The New Puzzle Classics

The Q-Grid Puzzle

Divide the wire grid shown above into three *congruent* parts.

The Shark Challenge

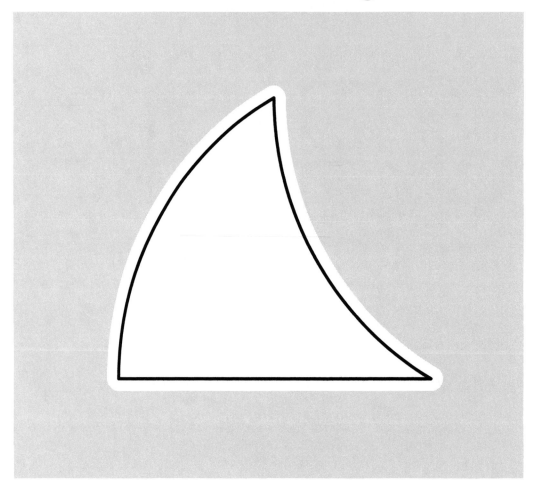

Using two straight lines, divide this figure into two parts of the same area.

Manta's Puzzle

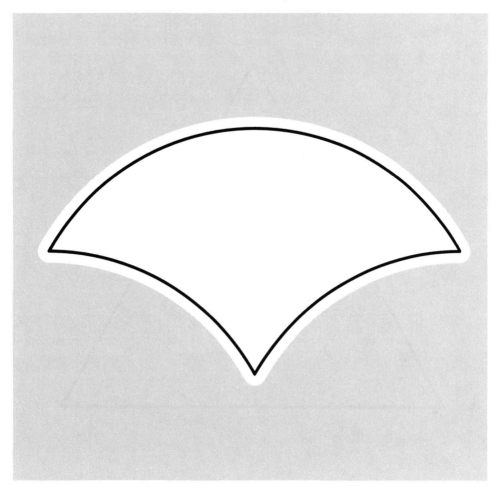

With four straight lines, divide this figure into three parts of the same area.

The Triangle Table Puzzle

A triangle table is inlaid with ten gold nails placed on the table as shown in the illustration. Can you divide the table into five parts of the same area, but *different* shapes, in such a way that every part will contain the same portion of gold nails?

Challenging Diamond

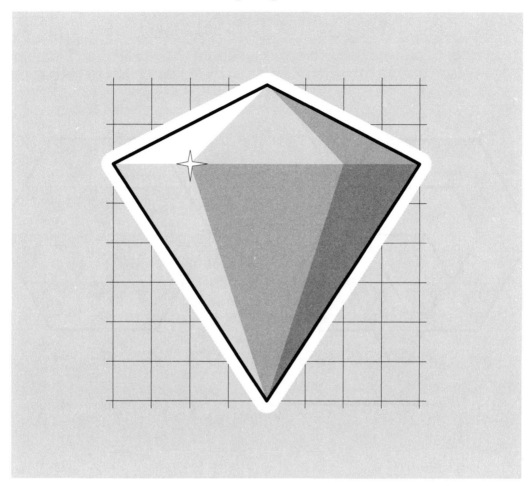

Divide the diamond into six *congruent* parts.

The Checkered Q

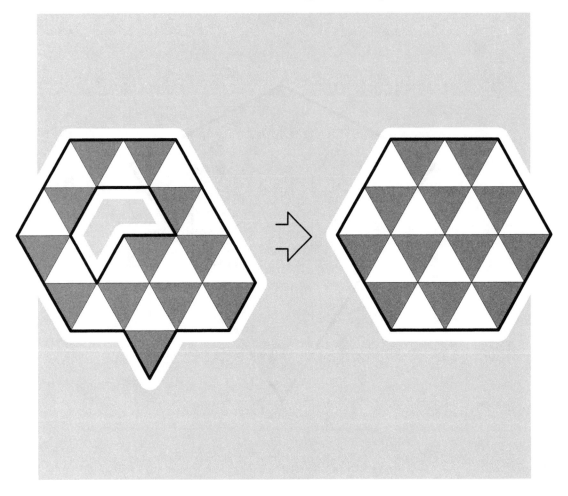

Divide the checkered Q-shape on the left into two pieces that can be rearranged into the checkered hexagon shown on the right.

Star & Cross

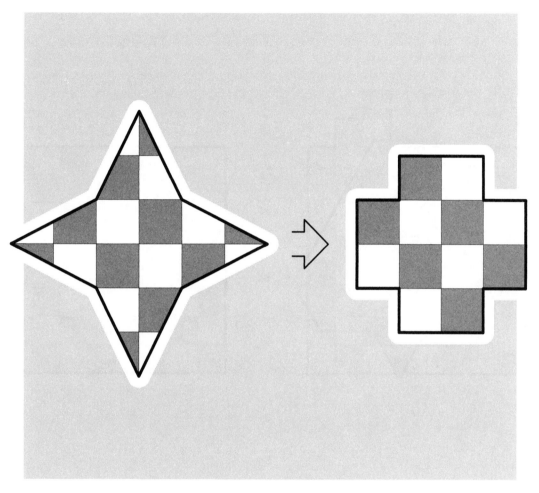

Divide the checkered star on the left into five pieces so that they can be rearranged into the checkered cross exactly as shown on the right.

Holes in a Checkerboard

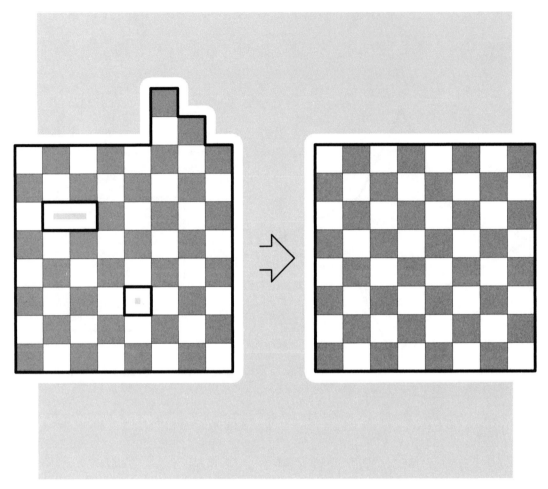

Divide the checkered shape on the left into two pieces that can be rearranged into the checkerboard shown on the right.

The New Puzzle Classics

Checkered Multiplication

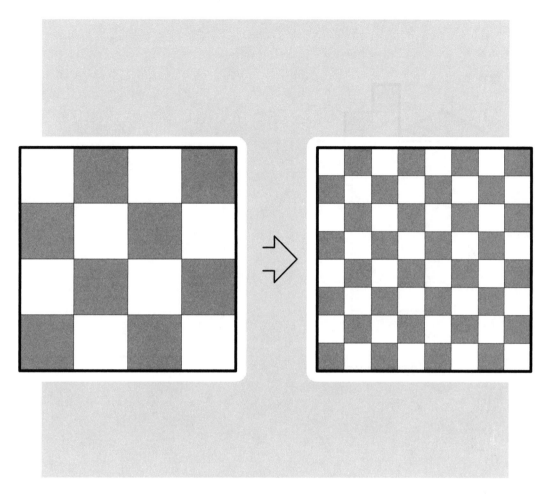

What is the minimum number of pieces needed to divide the 4 X 4 checkerboard shown on the left in order to assemble them into a "standard" 8 X 8 checkerboard like that shown on the right? How can it be done?

The Shield Challenge

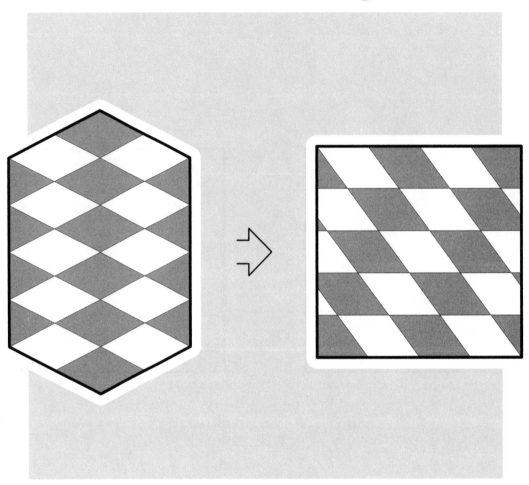

Divide the shield on the left into four pieces that can be rearranged into the square shown on the right. The pattern of the square must be exactly as shown.

Triangle Addition

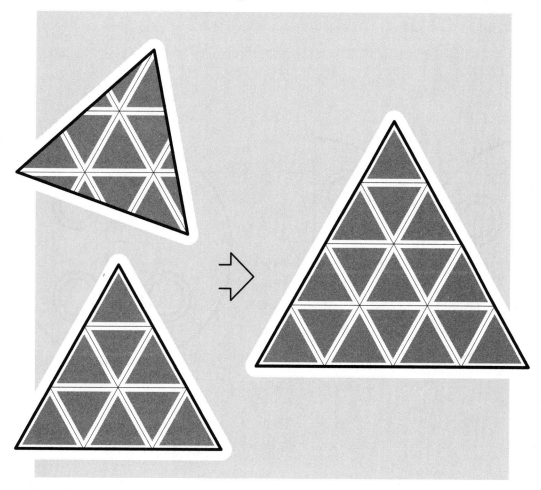

Cutting only along the lines, divide the pair of two smaller triangles shown on the left into five parts, and assemble them into one big triangle exactly as shown on the right.

Restore the Button

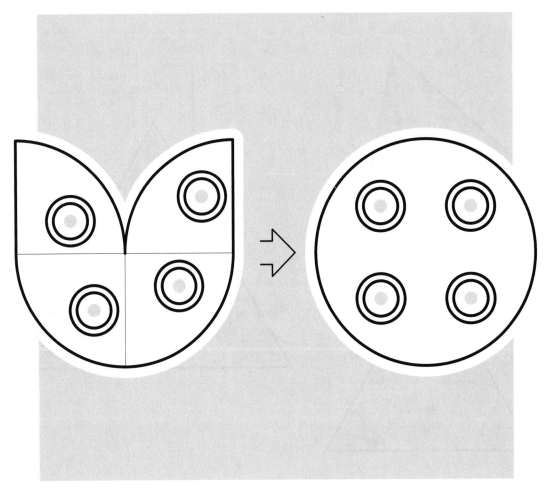

Divide the shape with four holes shown on the left into three parts, which can be rearranged into the circular button with its holes making a symmetric pattern, as shown on the right.

Molecular Dissection

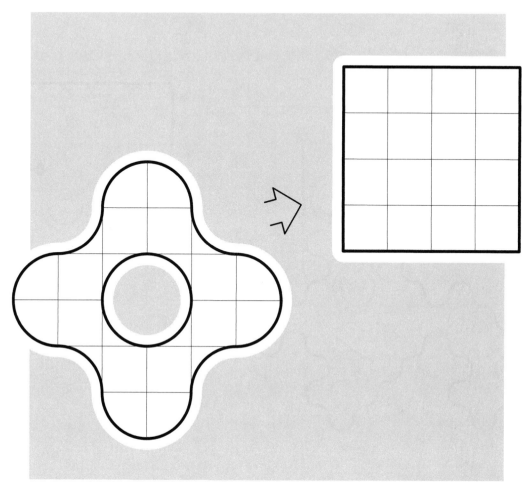

Divide the figure on the left into five *different* parts so that they may be rearranged into the square shown above right.

Dragon Squaring

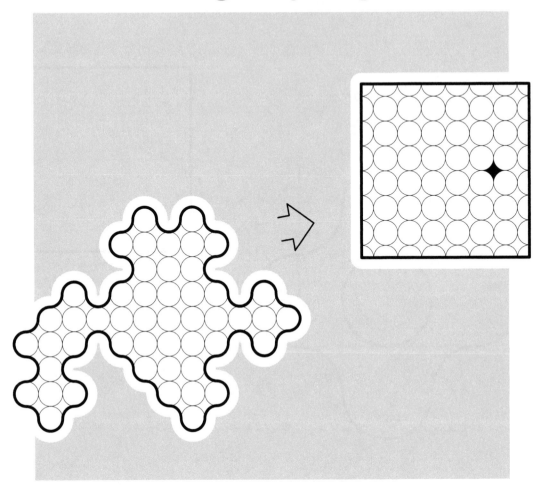

With three straight lines, divide the "dragon" shape shown on the left into four parts so that they can be rearranged into the square shown above right. The pattern of the square must be exactly as that shown. *Hint:* No piece will cover the small black spot on the square.

The New Puzzle Classics

The Pectoral Puzzle

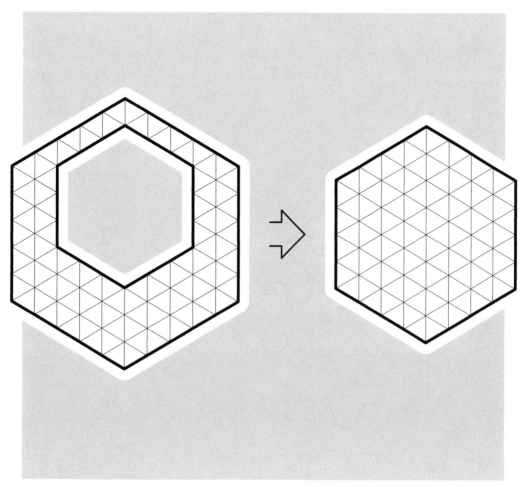

Divide the figure on the left into six *different* trapezoids that can be rearranged into the hexagon shown on the right.

Squaring the Arrow

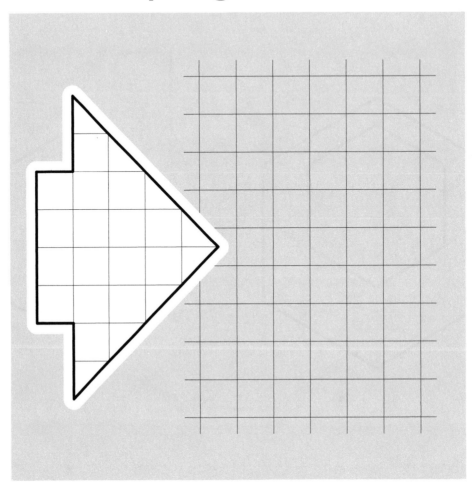

Divide the arrow shown above into four *different* shapes so that they can be assembled into two different squares. The grid on the right is provided to draw these squares.

The New Puzzle Classics

Christmas Tree & Square

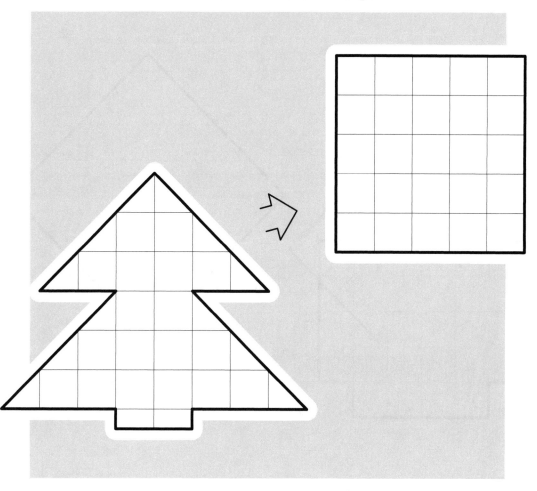

Divide the Christmas tree shape shown on the left into five *different* shapes so that they can be rearranged into the square shown above right. Note that its pattern may differ slightly from that shown.

Grid Changes

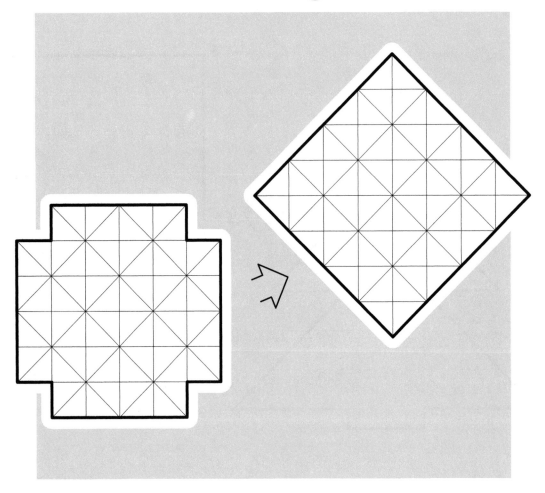

Divide the cross shown on the left into six *different* pieces and then rearrange them into the square shown above right. The pattern of the square must be exactly as that shown. You may cut only along the lines marked on the cross. *Hint:* None of the pieces rotate while reassembling into the square.

The New Puzzle Classics

Squared Eight

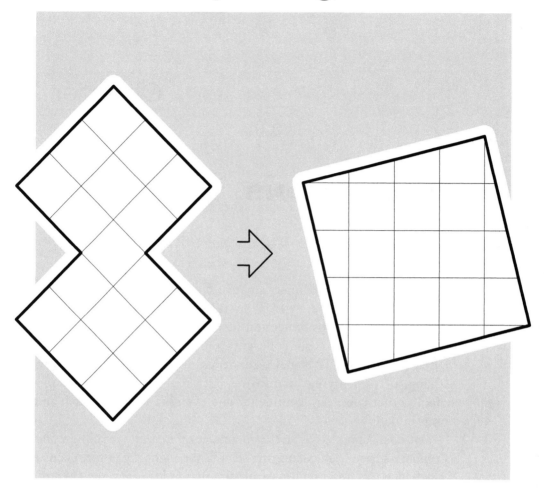

Divide the figure shown on the left into five *different* pieces so that they can be rearranged into the square shown on the right.

Chapter 2

DOT-CONNECTIONS

Every time we connect any two points—whether in space or on a sheet of paper, virtual or real—we, in fact, are solving the simplest dot-connection puzzle. Every day, when we call our friends and relatives, or our colleagues and bosses, we are making myriads of dot-connections. We make countless dot-connecting routes while walking, driving, flying, or moving between our homes, workplaces, schools, other countries, continents, and even between the Earth and far points in outer space.

Dot-connecting has always been a practical matter—recall how ancient astronomers have been connecting stars in the night sky to form constellations, which was important in many different fields of life such as agriculture, travel, navigation, and seasonal and cyclic events and rituals. A very complex form of dot-connecting is route planning, which utilizes core parts of control, management, and technological processes, and which ensures normal movements of traffic, subways, navigation, flights, pipelines, and journeys, to name just a few.

Dot-connecting was, and still is, an art. Again, different constellations and their mythological and poetic names are one great example of this. Connecting numbered dots to form pictures is a common form of art among young children.

Last but not least, dot-connections make for great puzzling. This chapter contains puzzles that try to reflect the infinite number of possible dot-connections by posing original challenges and illustrating the most traditional of these puzzles from a modern standpoint. You will find puzzles with different themes such as flowers and marbles, stars and spirals, bulbs in a vase, railroads connecting depots, common dominoes, contour tangrams, lines and strips, racetracks and matchstick connections, and other original dot-connecting challenges.

There are some rules that should be observed while you solve dot-connection puzzles. When solving challenges that involve connecting some sets of shapes with chains of straight lines, you should remember that:

1. All lines must always go through the centers of the respective points represented by different shapes—flowers, stars, spirals, marbles, and so forth.

2. Every route must be continuous. Its lines must make a chain, not necessarily closed in a loop. Every chain of the lines may turn at any point, including a shape itself (its central point).

3. The lines of the chain can cross each other, but never at any of the shapes.

4. No object on your route should be visited twice.

If you are given a set of some route's parts, you can rotate them as you wish, but you are not allowed to overturn and/or overlap them, unless stated otherwise.

The Flower Arrow

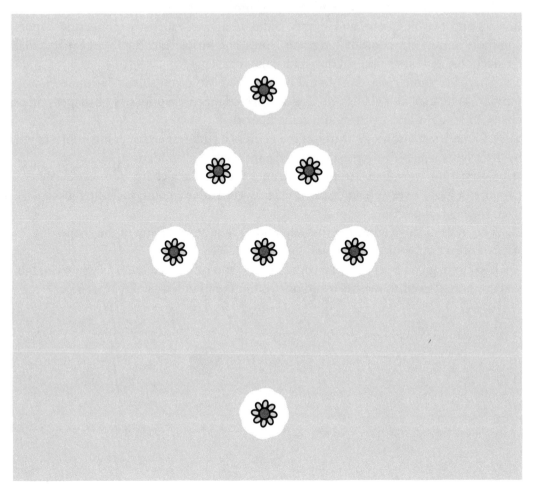

With three consecutive straight lines, connect all seven flowers so that every flower is passed through just once.

Join Eight Marbles

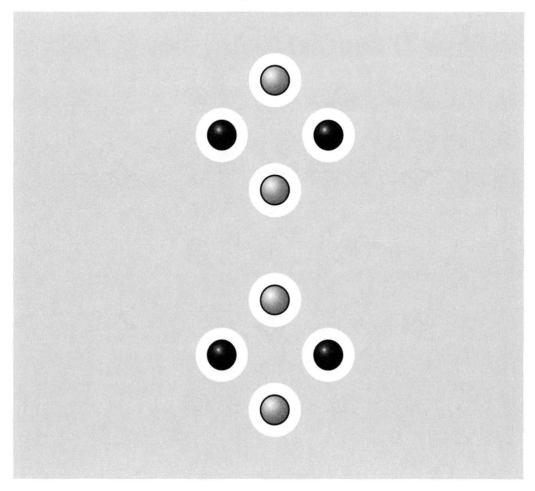

Draw exactly four consecutive straight lines so that they connect all eight marbles shown above. Every line must go through two marbles only—one light and one dark.

Stars & Spirals

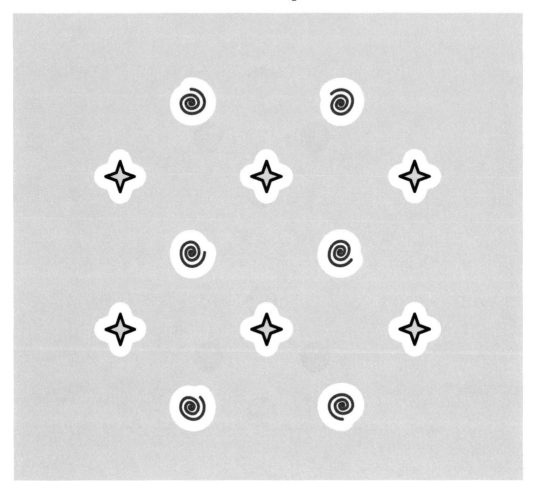

Link the six stars and six spirals with exactly five connected straight lines. Stars and spirals along your route must alternate (star. . . spiral. . . star. . . spiral. . . , etc.), and each of them must be visited just once.

The Puzzle Constellation

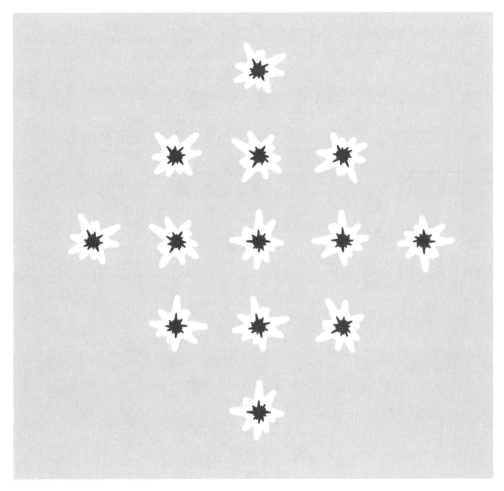

All thirteen stars that form the recently discovered constellation 2BY2-45-3BY3 shown above can be linked with exactly five connected straight lines. Can you solve this star challenge?

The Constellation of the Crescent

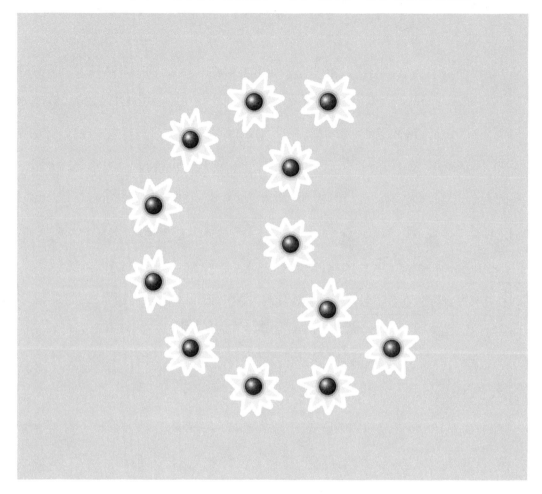

Can you link all twelve stars in the constellation of the crescent shown above with exactly five connected straight lines, going through every star just once?

The PUZZLE Connection

Link all nineteen letter balls in the big hexagon shown above with exactly seven connected straight lines, going through every letter ball just once. Note that letters along every single line must not repeat. As an added puzzle, how many different ways can you read PUZZLE by going through small neighboring hexagons with letter balls within the big hexagon?

In the Domino Mood

Can you cross all the pips on the "5-5" domino shown above with exactly four connected straight lines, going through every pip just once? You may cross the vertical short line that divides the domino into two halves. Can you also discover a *closed* route of four straight lines?

Dicey Connections

The object of this challenge is to connect the 4, 5, and 6 pips on the die shown in the central illustration above by using only nine straight connected lines, and going through each pip only once. Every line must belong to the respective face where it crosses a pip or pips placed on that face. At the same time, the ends of the lines can go into the space outside the die surface, and even connect there with one another. As an example, in the upper left diagram you can see how to connect the 1, 2, and 3 pips with just three straight connected lines.

Bouquet of Bulbs

Connect all five color clips placed inside the vase shown above with a bulb of the same color. No contact lines may cross each other or any clips. Also, the bulbs make a tight fit, but no contact lines may cross; since the bulbs touch each other tightly, you may only go around them. Note that the vase has just one opening at its top that you may use to go with lines outside it.

The New Puzzle Classics

Buttons, Needles & Threads

This puzzle consists of a big ring that holds three needles stuck into it. There are also three pairs of different buttons (with different numbers of holes in them). One button in each pair is glued to the ring, while the other one is placed within the ring. The ring with the needles and buttons is shown in the illustration above. The object of this puzzle is to connect the buttons in every pair with one, two, and three pieces of thread, respectively, depending on the number of thread ends joined to particular buttons. Every thread has to pass through the eye of only one needle, and it must do this exactly once. You are allowed to pass exactly two threads through every needle eye. Note that thread lines must neither cross each other nor themselves. Also, thread lines should not go over or under the ring, buttons, and needles, except at those places shown in the illustration.

As you can see, all beginnings and ends of threads, and three pairs of short pieces of thread passed through the needles' eyes—one pair per eye—are shown for your convenience. Now, your challenge is to properly connect all the thread pieces based on the conditions described above. And remember, the shorter the threads you use, the better puzzle tailor you are!

The Match Connections

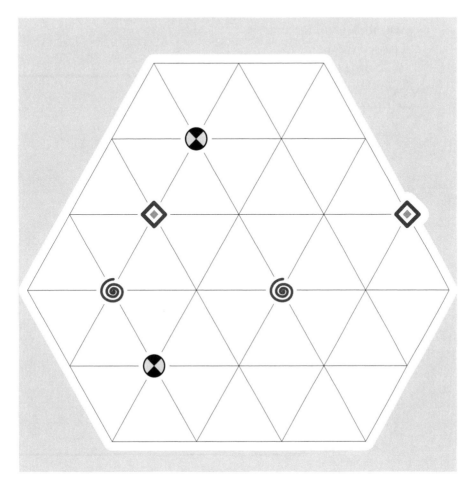

Connect matching signs into pairs using exactly eight matchsticks for every pair of signs. A matchstick is equal to the side of a single triangle cell of the grid. The matchstick paths must neither cross nor overlap one another or themselves. Paths must also not touch each other or themselves, even at a corner.

Arrowhead Connection

The general object of this puzzle is to connect the six triangles placed on the triangular grid above at right into three pairs of two triangles of the same color in every pair. All connecting lines—their segments—must run along the lines of the grid vertically and at 60-degree angles to its vertical. No crossing, self-crossing, or overlapping of the lines is allowed. The lines must also not touch each other or themselves, even at a corner.

Two triangles connected with a line to form a pair must always make two arrow heads, which in every pair must always aim in exactly *opposite directions*; a small sample of such a pair of connected triangles is shown in diagram A. At the end, you must have six arrowheads (connected into three pairs) aiming in six *different* directions as presented in diagram B. In other words, no two arrowheads may aim in the same direction.

Knight's Tetra-Connexions

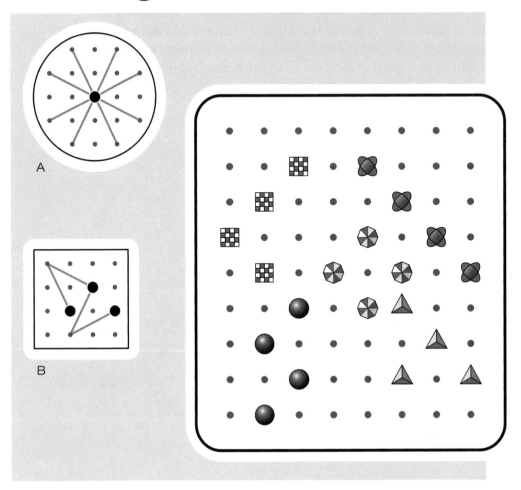

Each of the five groups of symbols placed on the board with an 8 X 9 grid of dots shown above at right is formed with four equal shapes. Actually, these groups represent five different tetraminoes. The object of this puzzle is to connect all four shapes within every group into a chainlike o--o--o--o by performing chess knight's moves. Each of the six line segments in the chain represents one move, considering every leap of the knight as a straight segment. All possible knight's moves from a dot are shown in diagram A.

All five chains must be separate, and they must not cross or touch each other at any point. Every line segment must run just from dot to dot, and they should neither cross each other nor run through any shapes that belong to the other chains placed on the board. Shapes within a chain may be connected in any order. A small example of how three dots can be connected into a chain o--o--o with four non-crossing knight leaps is shown in diagram B.

The Billiard Ball Trap Challenge

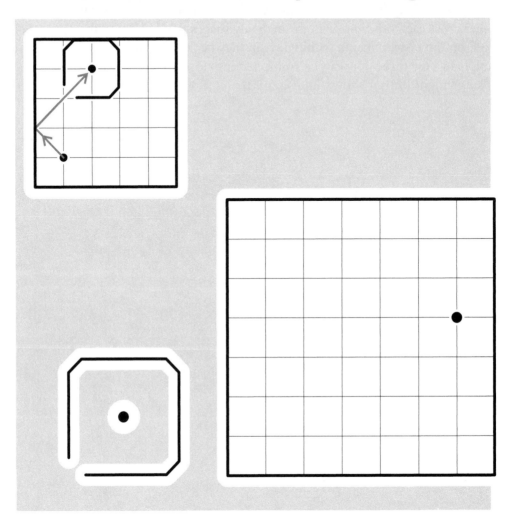

This puzzle consists of a 7 X 7 billiard table, a billiard ball, and a special 3 X 3 ball trap that looks like a C-shaped square frame with one entrance at its corner and a catching point at its center, shown above. When a billiard ball is struck, it starts to move in the direction of the stroke, and moves across the table in a straight line until it hits any obstacle, which in this puzzle are the table sides or the sides of the ball trap. Then the ball bounces off the obstacle and continues to move in another direction, and so on.

The New Puzzle Classics

For this puzzle, we will use a billiard rule (applied in math studies of billiards), that the angle of reflection after bouncing from an obstacle equals the angle of incidence. In this puzzle, the ball is always sent at a 45-degree angle from its start point, and its trajectory after any and all bounces runs at a 45-degree angle to the sides of the table and the ball trap. Bear in mind that if the ball hits any of the three truncated corners of the ball trap (or gets to a corner of the table) it will bounce directly back. The small example of a 5 X 5 table with a small 2 X 2 ball trap within it is shown in the uppermost left diagram. As you can see, the ball bounces once from the side of the table, and then enters the 2 X 2 ball trap, where it remains caught.

The object of the puzzle is to place the 3 X 3 ball trap within the 7 X 7 table so that a ball shown on the table, when sent in one of the four diagonal directions, will be caught within the ball trap after exactly *five bounces* (counting from both the table sides and the ball trap). You are allowed to rotate the ball trap 90, 180, or 270 degrees before you place it on the table, and its sides must coincide with the lines of the table grid. The ball trap remains unmoved after you place it on the table.

The Unicursal Tangram Bird

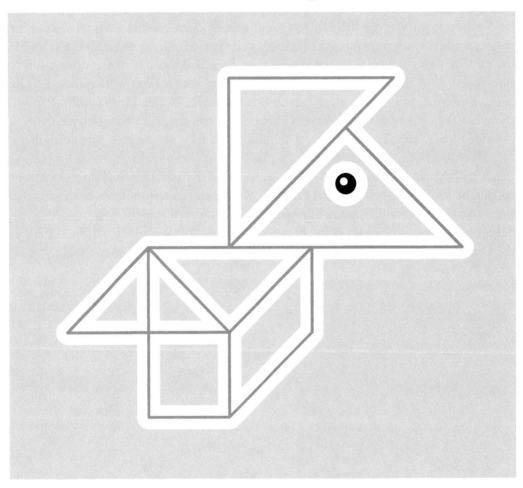

This unusual bird was build up of the seven tans of the contour tangram. Your goal is to find two points on its lines—start and finish—and then connect them with a continuous line running along each of the bird's lines exactly once. The line can touch, but not cross, itself.

The Double Unicursal Grid

The grid shown above consists of exactly two equal smaller grids, each of which can be drawn with one continuous line without lifting your pencil off the paper. You are not allowed to go twice along any of the lines' parts, cross the lines of different grids, or make self-crossings within any single line. Note that the two smaller grids may be mirror images of each other.

The Dragon Circuit

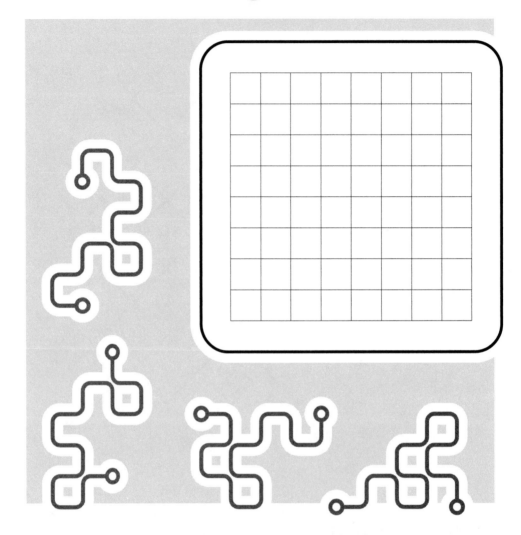

Connect the four wires presented above into a closed circuit (like a loop) within the 8 X 8 circuit plate shown above right. The wires must link with one another with the small clips at their ends only, and must neither cross nor touch each other. You may not bend or fold the wires, but you may rotate and flip them over.

The Seven Depots Puzzle

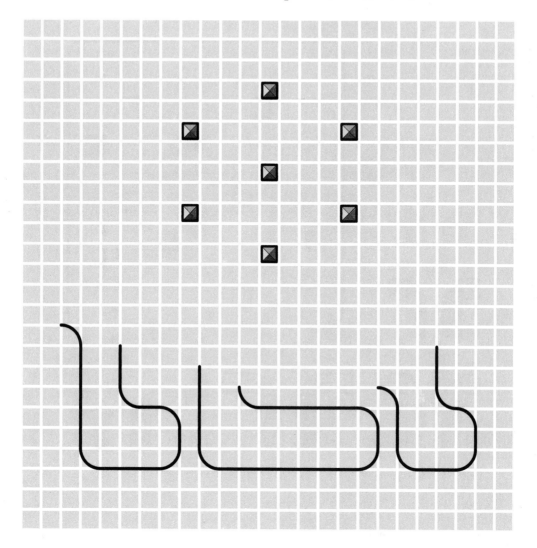

Assemble the three railroad parts into one closed loop (without self-crossing) that will connect all seven depots in one closed route. A depot to be connected to the route must touch at least one *straight* part of the railroad. You may rotate and overturn railroad parts, but you must neither overlap nor bend/fold them. Also they must not cross each other.

The Twisting Paper Snake

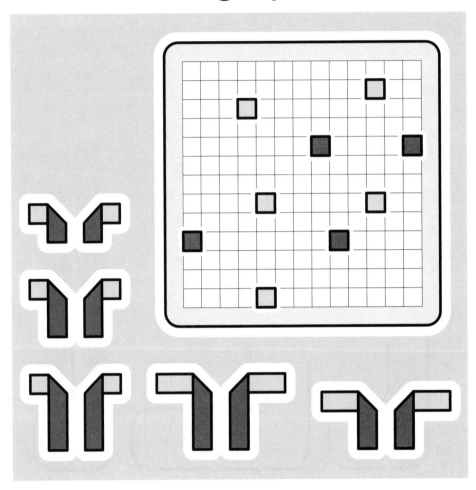

Ten two-colored paper strips were folded into the paper corners shown above. The challenge is to use all these pieces to assemble one continuous paper snake creeping (without self-crossing) over the grid shown above right.

The nine small squares in two colors placed on the grid represent fragments of the paper snake; the snake must go through all these fragments. Only two corners may be joined for each fragment, and the end of the corner that touches the fragment must be the same color as the fragment. None of the fragments may be covered with corners, and the snake must not make turns at any of the fragments. You may rotate and turn over the corners, but you may not overlap or unfold them. The final snake must be fully placed within the grid.

The Racetrack Puzzle

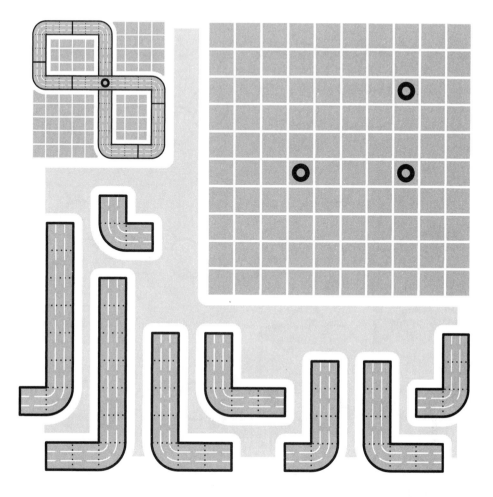

With the eight L-fragments shown above, the object of the puzzle is to build up a racetrack within a 10 X 10 area (shown at upper right) using all eight fragments. A sample of a racetrack built up of six fragments within a 10 X 10 area is shown in the uppermost left diagram. The final track must make a loop with all its outside corners rounded. The track can cross itself, and its intersections should look as if the track goes over itself. At the same time, keep in mind that all fragments of the track *lie in one layer*, and in the intersections they form something like an image of a bridge; the sample track has one such intersection, marked with a circle. No flipping or overlapping of the fragments is allowed. *Hint:* All intersections of the final racetrack are shown in the 10 X 10 area on the right.

The Color Candy Chain

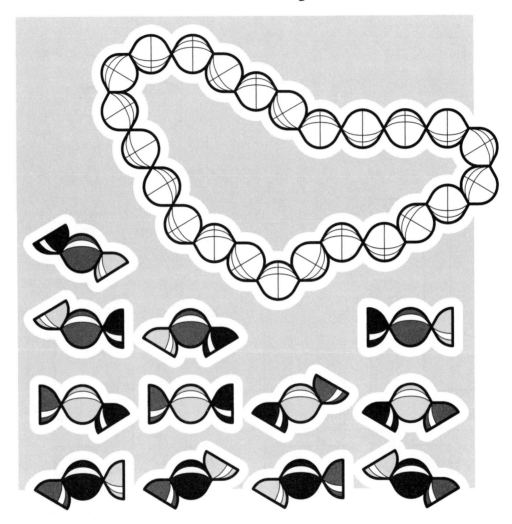

The twelve multicolored candies scattered above can be joined together into the closed chain—shown in the uppermost illustration—so that they form twenty-four whole candy balls—eight in each of the three colors. Can you crack this sweet challenge, and define the exact place of every candy in the chain? Bear in mind that the candies are shown as they should be used in the chain—you may not fold their ends to change their configuration, nor may you overlap or flip them over, but you may rotate them as you wish.

The Challenge of the Green Line

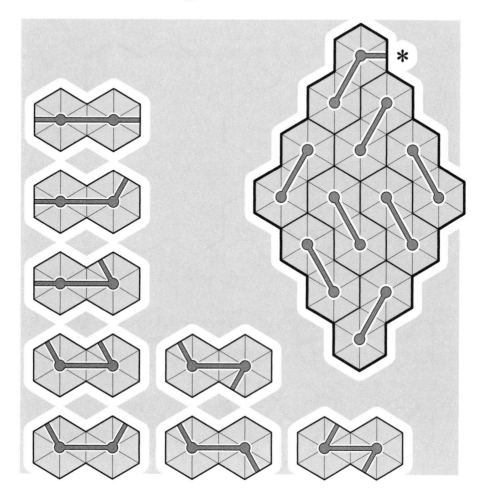

The eight domino-like pieces shown above can be arranged to form the rhombic comb shown on the right so that one continuous line appears. The line must begin and end on the periphery of the comb. One of its ends is marked with an asterisk at the top of the comb. As you can see, the outlines of all eight pieces and some fragments of the lines are already shown on the comb. Your challenge is to find the other end of the green line and draw its final apearance. Note that pieces are transparent, and any of them may be flipped over; in this case, you will see the same piece with its pattern symmetric to the pattern on the other side.

The Color Comb Zigzag

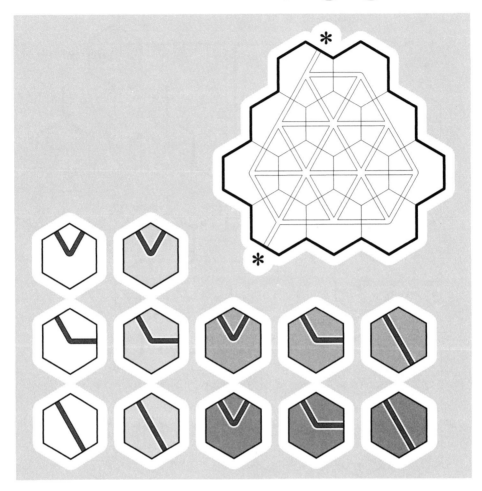

The twelve hexagonal pieces in four colors can be placed within the comb shape above to form a single continuous zigzag line connecting the two asterisks next to the borders of the comb shape. How can it be done? Note that no two hexagons of the same color may touch each other. The grid within the shape is shown for drawing the final zigzag line, which should run just within this grid.

Lines-Through-Dots

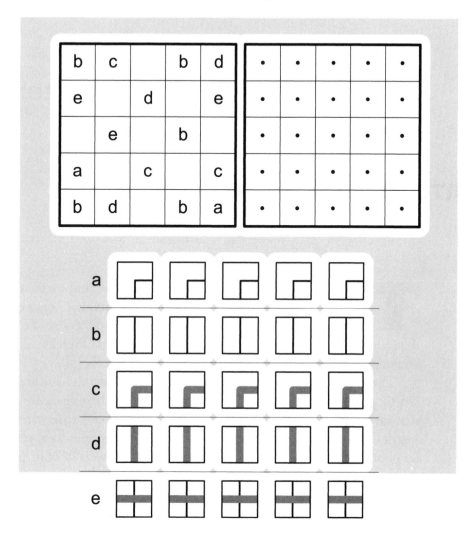

Place all twenty-five squares (a–e) with line fragments within the right 5 X 5 grid so that they form several continuous lines—thin and thick—running through all twenty-five dots of the right grid. Every line must begin and end on the border of the grid. Each letter in the left grid indicates which of the line fragments lies in the corresponding cell of the right grid. But the letters do not show the exact orientation of the lines; that is for you to determine. Note that you may rotate the squares as you wish.

Chapter 3

MATCHSTICKS & COINS

This chapter contains puzzles of two different kinds, which can be defined as composing puzzles with elements that may be found almost anywhere: namely, matchsticks and coins. For most matchstick puzzles, matches may be replaced with toothpicks. Similarly, counters may be used for many coin puzzles.

These two kinds of puzzles are mostly classified as mechanical puzzles, but they are even more than that—they forge a link between pure mathematical puzzles—geometrical and combinatorial—and true mechanical puzzles. Perhaps this is the main reason why these puzzles have remained so popular but at the same time rare enough (especially coin puzzles) over many centuries. And many of these are now true classics, part of puzzledom's treasures.

Other puzzles with matchsticks and coins are incorporated into several other chapters of this book, such as puzzles with matchsticks forming challenging match snakes, and coins moving on special grids.

Matchstick Puzzles

There are some general rules that should be applied to all matchstick puzzles, unless otherwise stated:

1. There are no loose ends of matchsticks used in puzzles; in other words, the entire length of matchsticks must be used.

2. Matchsticks must not overlap each other.

3. You are not allowed to break and/or bend matchsticks;

4. Remember that matchsticks in all puzzles are used as math segments of length 1.

5. The lines within some shapes are provided to show their proportions for your convenience. Unless it is specified in the instructions to a particular puzzle, you may use these lines as you wish, or not at all.

Coin Puzzles

There are also some rules to observe while solving coin puzzles that transform some shapes into other ones. (For these puzzles, the start and final positions are always shown.) These rules are as follows:

1. Light and dark circles always represent different sides of coins.

2. Every single coin, after it is moved, must touch at least two coins from the unmoved group. This rule ensures an exact position of the moved coin in its new place. Some basic legal and illegal moves are shown in the diagrams below:

Legal Moves   Illegal Move

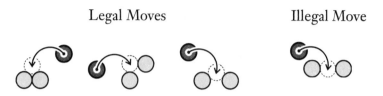

3. Every final pattern (formed with light and dark circles) must be oriented exactly as it is shown in the corresponding diagram always placed on the right;

4. The final pattern need not necessarily be formed exactly where the start pattern was located.

For other coin puzzles (with just start shapes) you do not have to apply the above rules.

Cat & Chair

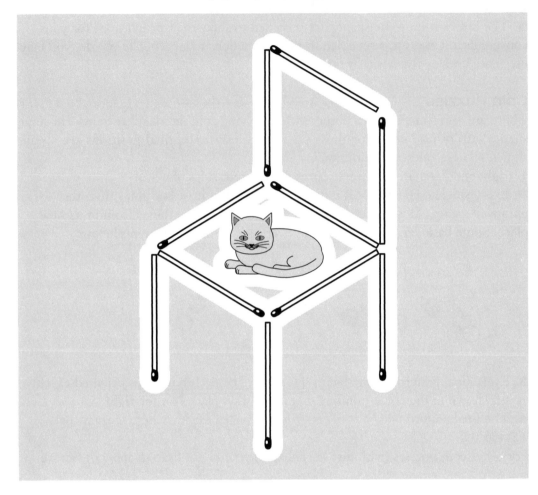

Move four matchsticks to get the cat under the chair.

Squares in the Window

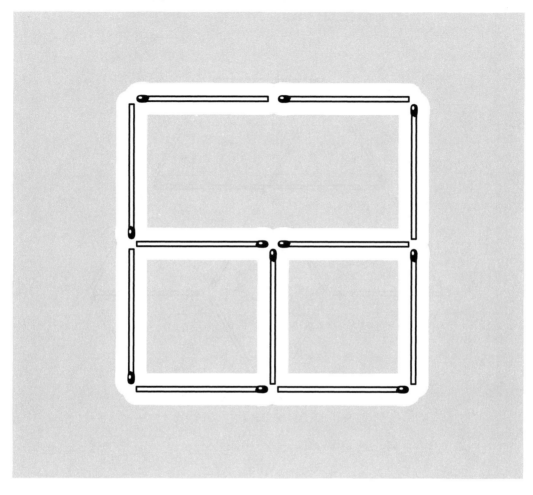

This window contains three squares, counting those of different sizes. Move four matchsticks so that four squares appear.

Not One Rhombus

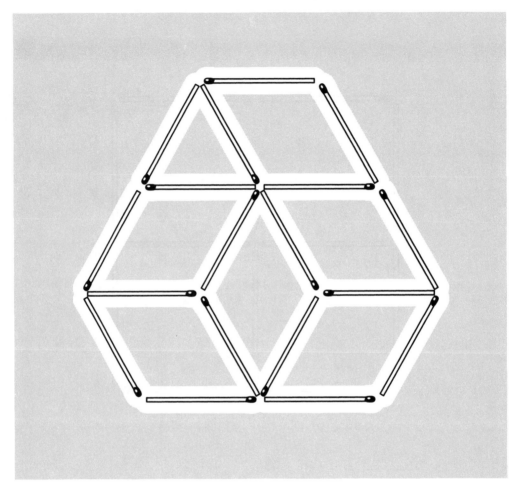

The figure above contains six rhombuses. What is the minimum number of match-sticks that need to be removed so that no rhombuses remain?

The Flying Bird

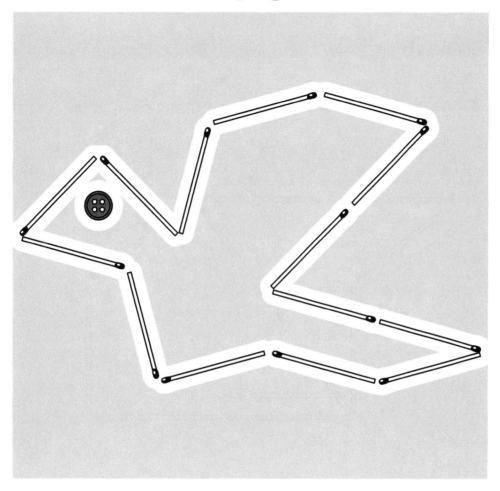

Move eight matchsticks and the button to make the bird fly in the other direction.

Two Matching Areas

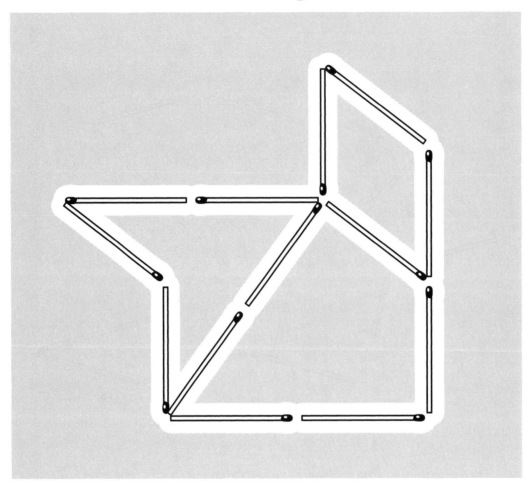

The above shape is divided into three different areas. Move three matchsticks to form one shape divided into exactly two equal parts with the same area and shape; they may be mirror images of each other.

Match Similarity

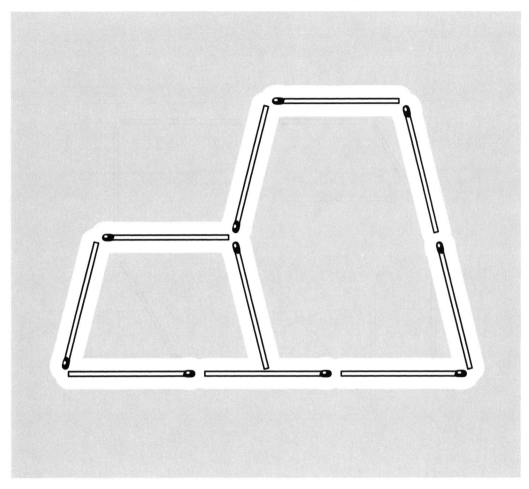

This shape is divided into two nonsimilar parts. Move two matchsticks to form a shape divided into two similar parts which may not necessarily be of the same size. In other words, these two regions must be mutually proportionate with respect to their sides and angles.

Skew Rectangle

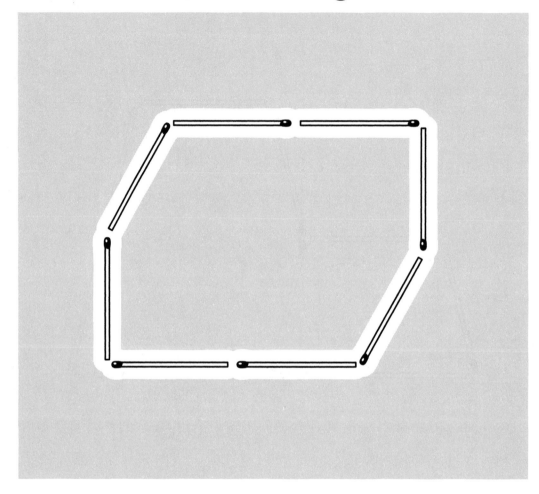

Move four matchsticks to make a figure that contains exactly half of the area of the original figure.

Square & Division

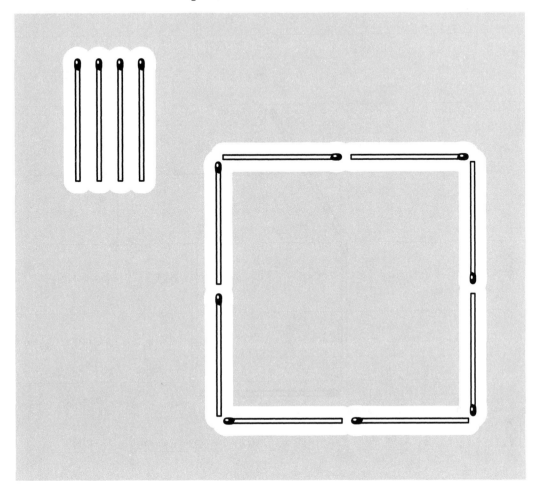

Divide this square with four matchsticks to form:
1. Two parts of the same area and shape.
2. Three parts of the same area and shape.

The Cottage

Divide this cottage into two parts with the same area using:

1. One matchstick.
2. Two matchsticks.
3. Three matchsticks.
4. Four matchsticks.

The New Puzzle Classics

The Shoe

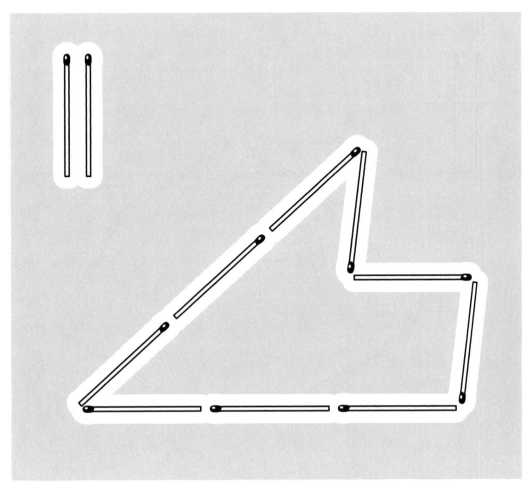

Divide this shoe with two matchsticks to form two parts of the same area.

The Marquee

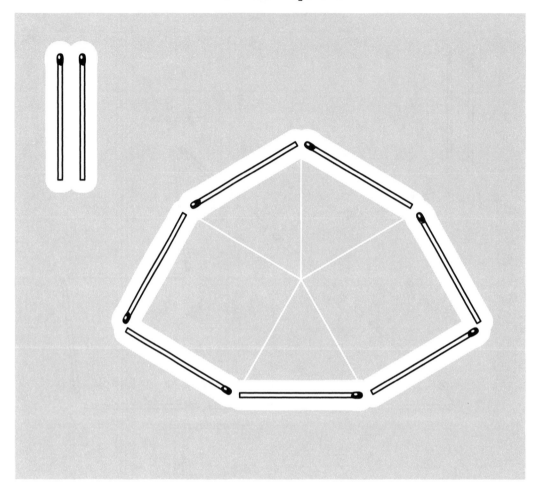

Divide the marquee with two matchsticks to form two parts of the same area.

Trisection of Octagon

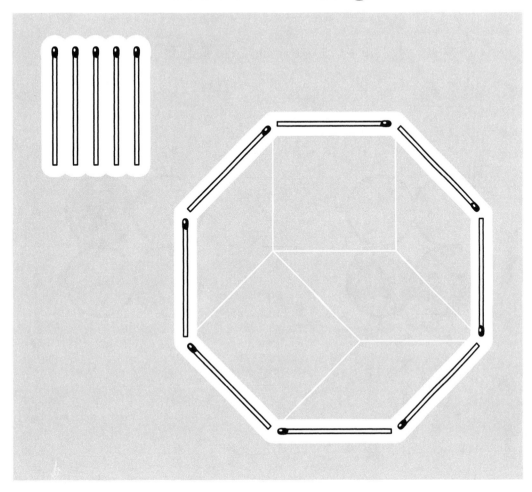

Divide the octagon above with five matchsticks to form three parts of the same area.

Quadragonal

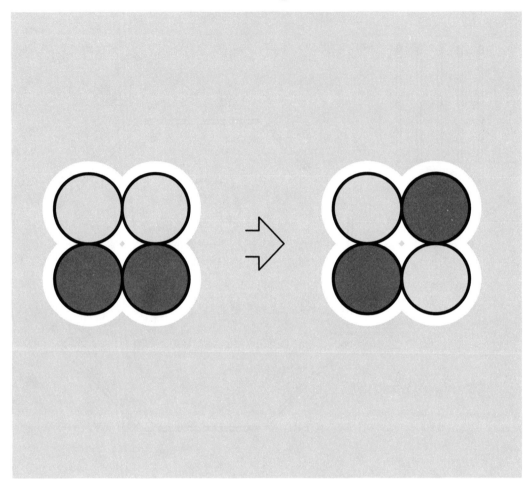

Place four coins as shown in the left diagram. Moving one coin at a time, form the pattern on the right in just four single moves.

Redirect the Corner

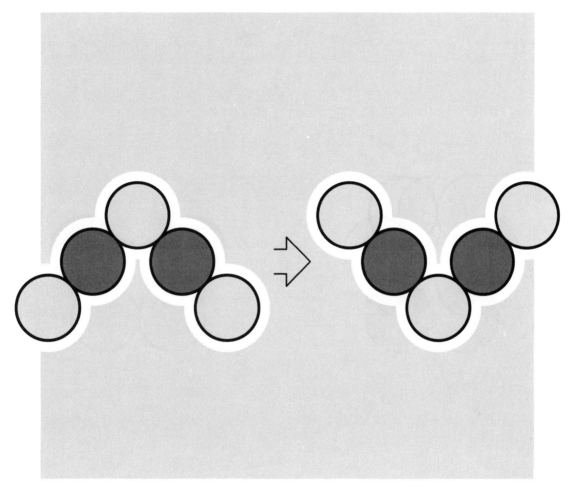

Place five coins to form a corner, as shown in the diagram at left. Now, moving one coin at a time, redirect the corner (as shown in the right diagram) in four single moves.

The Penta-Coin Change

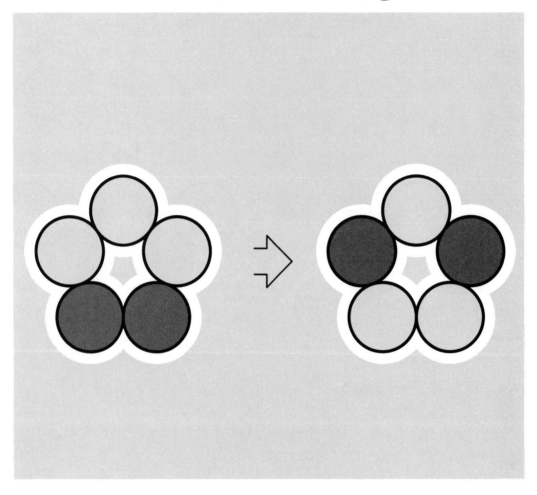

Five coins form a regular pentagon as shown in the left diagram. Move one coin at a time to create the pattern on the right in just five single moves.

Turn Up the Shell

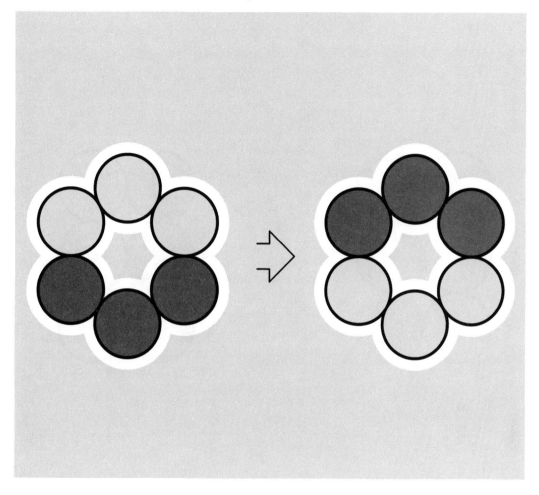

Six coins form a shell as shown in the left diagram. Move one coin at a time to create the pattern on the right in just six single moves.

Vertical Flip-Flop

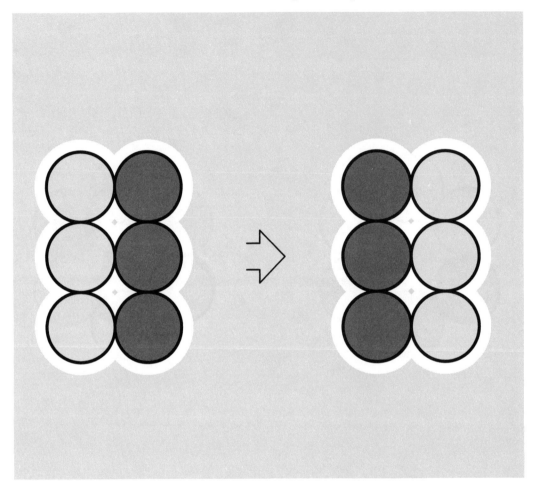

Place six coins as shown in the left diagram. Move one coin at a time to create the pattern on the right in just five single moves.

The New Puzzle Classics

Slide the Row

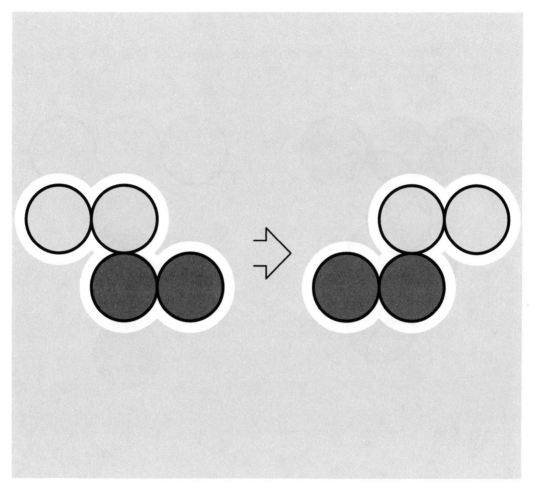

Place four coins as shown in the left diagram. Move one coin at a time so that the coins form the position shown on the right in seven single moves.

The T-Coin Challenge

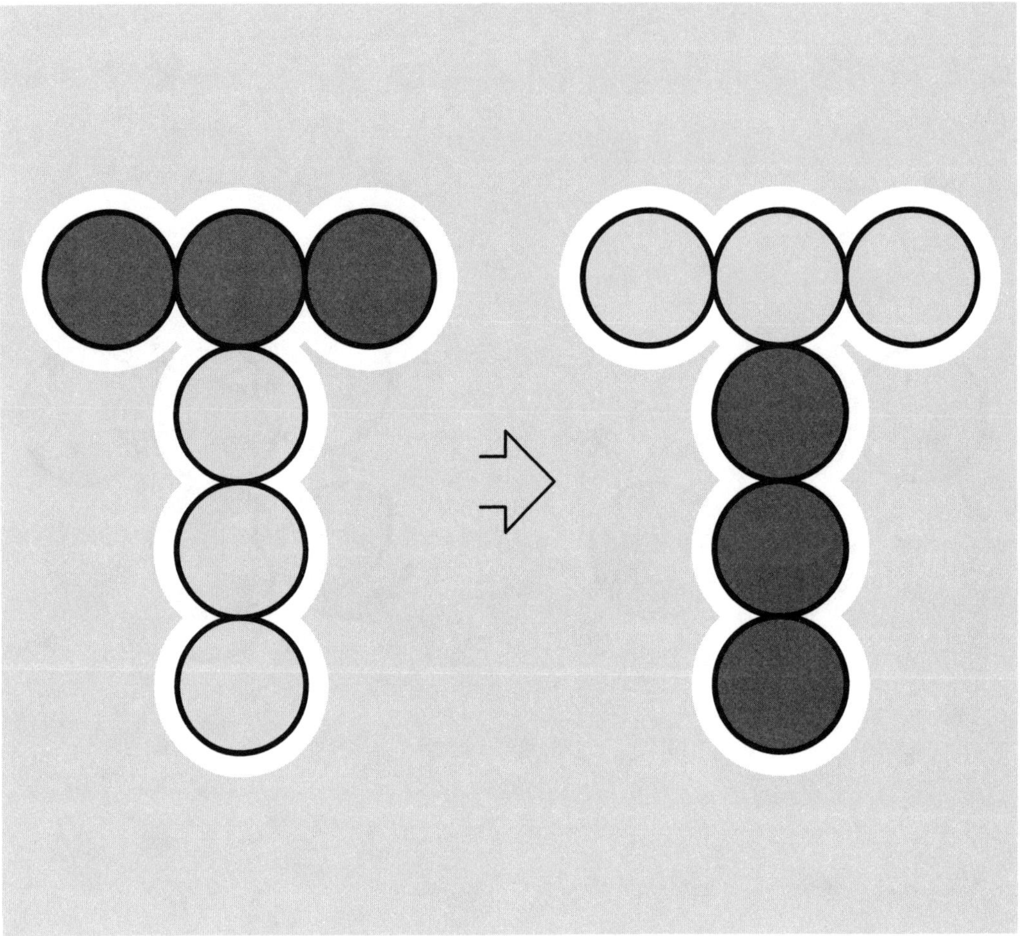

The T on the left is made up of six coins. Moving one coin at a time, exchange the original T's horizontal and vertical parts, to change it into another T (shown at right) in eight single moves.

Hexa-Flower

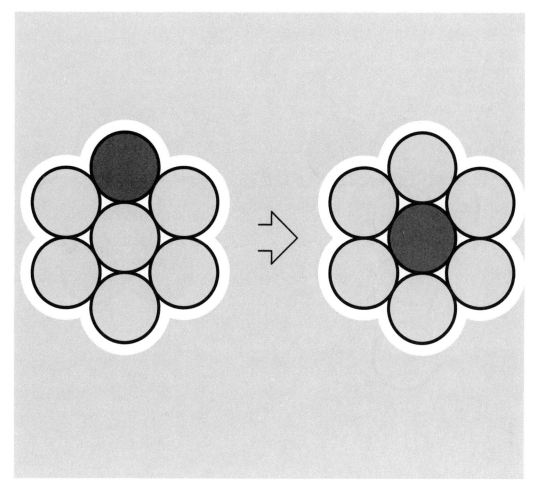

Seven coins make a flower as shown in the diagram at left. You may move any pair of adjacent coins to another position so that it will touch the unmoved group; every time at least one triad (a small triangle consisting of three coins touching each other) appears. Such a triad must include one or both coins from the pair you have just moved. While moving a pair, you may not rotate it, and you must move it parallel to its start position. The object of the puzzle is to create the pattern on the right in just three moves of coin pairs.

Change Coin Rows

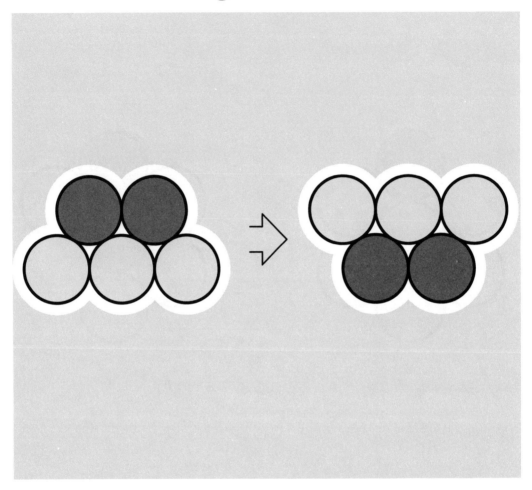

Place five coins as shown in the diagram at left. You may move any adjacent "light-dark" pair of coins to another position so that it will touch the unmoved group; every time at least one triad (a small triangle consisting of three coins touching each other) appears. Such a triad must include one or both coins from the pair that you have just moved. While moving a pair, you may not rotate it, and you must move it parallel to its start position. The object of the puzzle is to create the pattern on the right in six moves of coin pairs.

The New Puzzle Classics

Triads

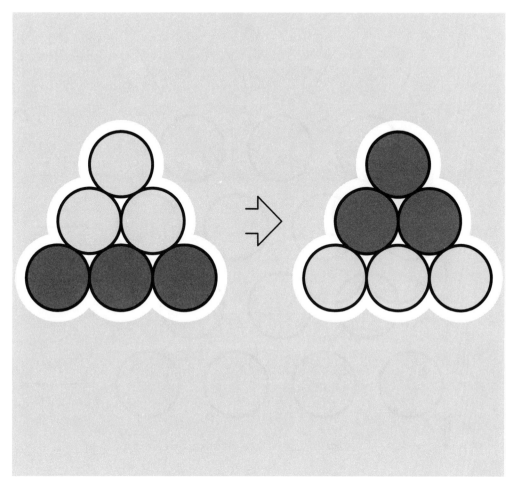

Place six coins as shown in the diagram at left. You may move any coin triad (a small triangle consisting of three coins touching each other) to another position so that this triad will touch the unmoved group, and every time at least one new triad appears. Every new triad must include one or two coins from the triad you have just moved. While moving a triad, you may not rotate it, and you must move it parallel to its start position. The object of the puzzle is to create the pattern on the right just in three moves of coin triads.

Twelve Rows of Coins

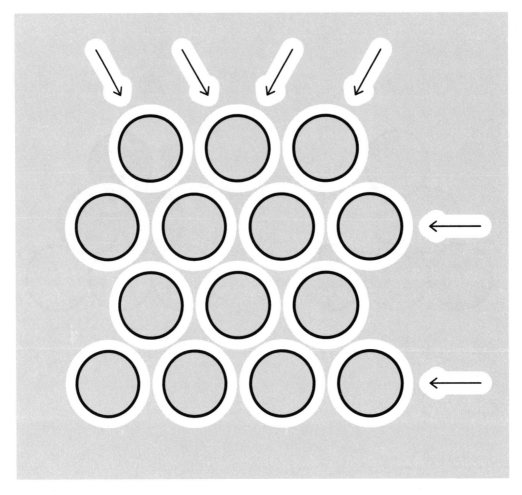

Place fourteen coins so that they form six rows containing four coins each as shown in the illustration above. The six rows are shown with arrows. Move just two coins to new positions to form twelve rows of four coins each.

The New Puzzle Classics

Four Coin Squares

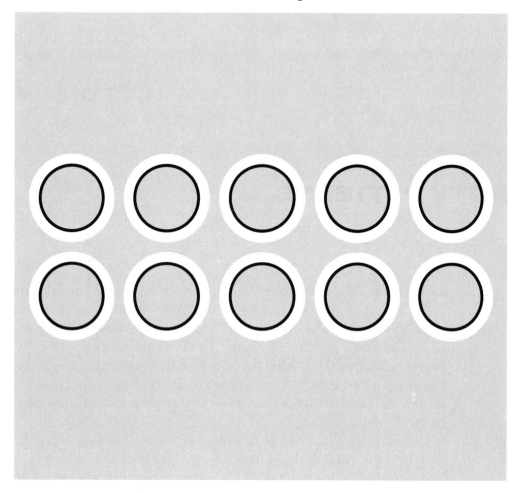

Ten coins are placed in two rows as shown above. As you can see, these coins form four coin squares of the same size. A coin square is formed when the centers of four coins lie at corners of a square of some size that can be oriented orthogonally, or turned at some angle. The object of the puzzle is to move three coins so that in a new composition all ten coins will form *only four squares* again, but this time these squares must be of *different* sizes. In other words, no pair of squares of the same size can be found in the new composition.

Chapter 4

WITTY PATTERNS

The challenges presented in this chapter are of the puzzle types that commonly appear at the World Puzzle Championships (WPCs). The first type can be defined as "self-containing grid-and-piece pencil puzzles"; the other I call "visual pattern puzzles." Of course, neither of these definitions can be fully associated jsut with these puzzle types, as they may also be applied to describe other types of puzzles as well. But these definitions describe the core properties of these puzzle types.

These puzzles may be also described as "pattern puzzles," since their grids (and the pieces in them) form patterns, and the object of these challenges is either to restore the whole pattern by putting pieces in a grid observing certain rules, or to distinguish and mark certain pieces hidden within a grid.

Grid-and-Pieces

To solve these puzzles you will need to analyze what you have: the puzzle grid's size and shape; the pieces and their number, color, and shape; and specific marks placed on the pieces and/or grids, such as numbers or letters, pictures or patterns, and their color and shape. Each of these properties contains important information that will help you to solve these puzzles.

There is another group of puzzles with clues specifically placed either around or within their grids. These clues, combined with certain rules and constraints described in the puzzle instructions, provide additional hints which will lead you along the solving process. It is very important to start by seeking unique places where certain pieces can be placed at the beginning with certainty. Step by step, you may continue to solve every particular puzzle with a reduced number of pieces, as well as additional clues you have gained at previous steps, and so on. This is one of the most effective approaches to solving these puzzles.

Visual Patterns

Two main points will be helpful in solving these challenges: first, systematic analysis, search, and recording of your results; second, careful observation and counting.

The Waffle Puzzle

The waffle shown above right is formed with the six pieces (shown to the left and below the waffle) placed within the shaded rectangle frame. Can you show how it was done? The pieces may be rotated, but you may not turn them over.

The New Puzzle Classics

Four Arrows

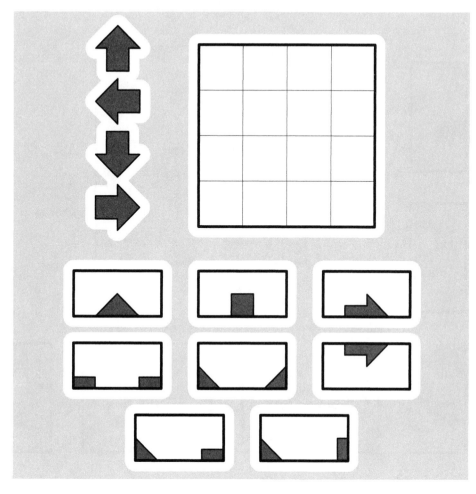

Place all eight rectangles into the 4 X 4 square (shown above right) so that four whole arrows appear. The arrows should be aimed in four different directions—up, down, left, and right; their orientation is shown at the upper left. You may rotate the rectangles, but you may neither turn them over nor overlap them.

Checkered Rectangles

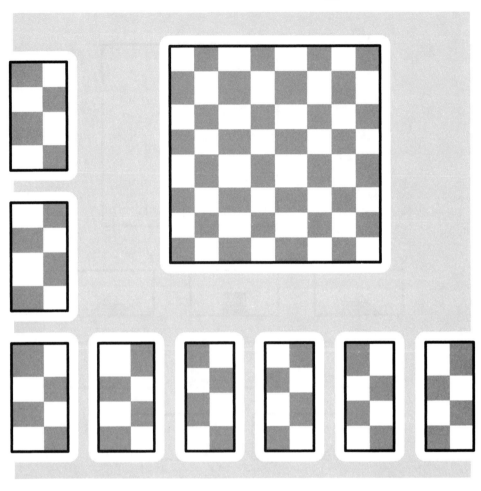

The 8 X 8 checkerboard shown above is made from the eight pieces shown below it and to its left. How can all of the pieces be placed within the checkerboard? Draw the lines between them. The pieces may be rotated, but you may neither overlap nor turn them over.

The Tangrammed Checkerboard

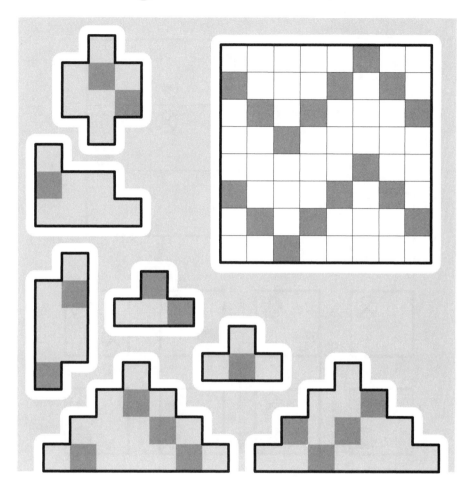

Place the seven transparent pieces shown above into a square so that they form the pattern exactly like that shown in the square diagram (top right). To solve the puzzle, draw the outlines of the pieces directly in the diagram. Keep in mind that you may rotate the pieces and flip them over as you wish, but you may not overlap them.

Squared Color Spots

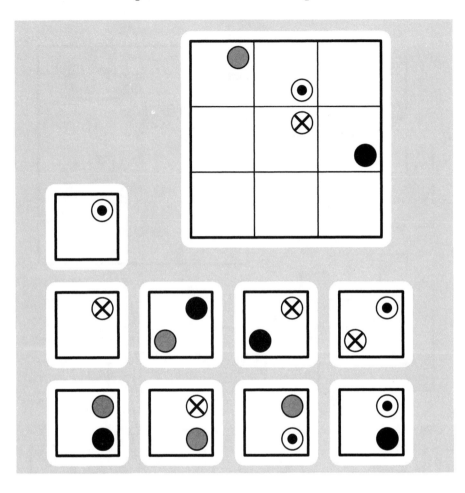

Place the nine pieces with colored spots shown above into the 3 X 3 grid (above right) so that every group of four spots of the same color and pattern forms a square. A square is formed when the centers of four spots lie at corners of a square of some size which may be oriented orthogonally, or turned at some angle. You may rotate the pieces as you wish, but you may neither overturn nor overlap them. *Hint:* One spot from every square is already shown within the 3 X 3 square in its correct place.

The New Puzzle Classics

The Bermuda Pearls

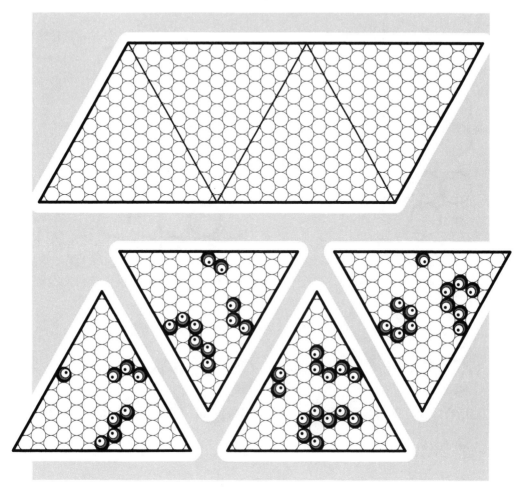

Using the four triangles shown above, form a parallelogram like the one in the uppermost illustration so that you can form nine chains of pearls ranging in length from one to nine pearls. Keep in mind that none of the chains should include three consecutive pearls in a straight line like the following: OOO.

Tetra-Marbles

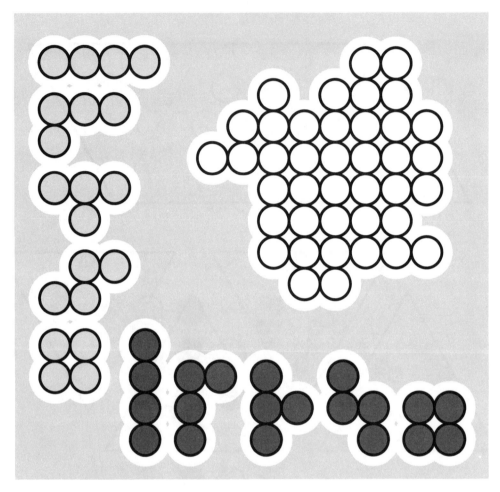

The irregular shape shown above at right was assembled out of the ten tetra-marble pieces shown next to and below it. Can you show how it was done, with every piece placed within the shape? Bear in mind that no two pieces of the same color and/or shape may touch each other. You may rotate and turn the pieces over, but they may not overlap.

The New Puzzle Classics

The Molecular Chain Puzzle

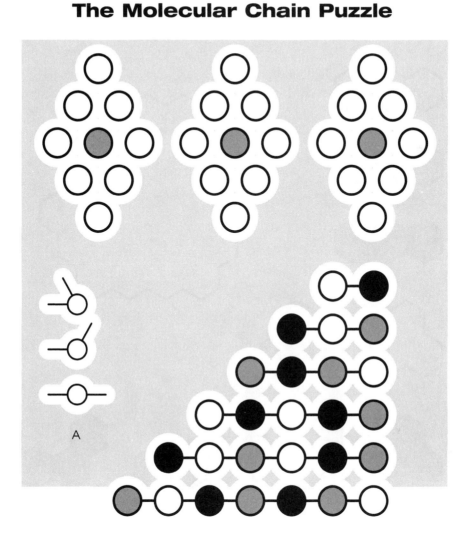

A

Assemble the six molecular chains shown below the three rhombuses presented in the uppermost illustration so that their molecules will form three identical color patterns; no matter how the treads that connect molecules in the chains will go through the rhombuses. In other words, if you superimpose all the rhombuses in the orientation as they are shown (with no turning), their color patterns should exactly match. Note that the threads of the chains are nonstretch, and at the chains' turns they may form junctions as shown in diagram A. Also, no parts of chains may overlap each other. The position of one molecule is already shown in each rhombus.

Hexa Three-by-Three

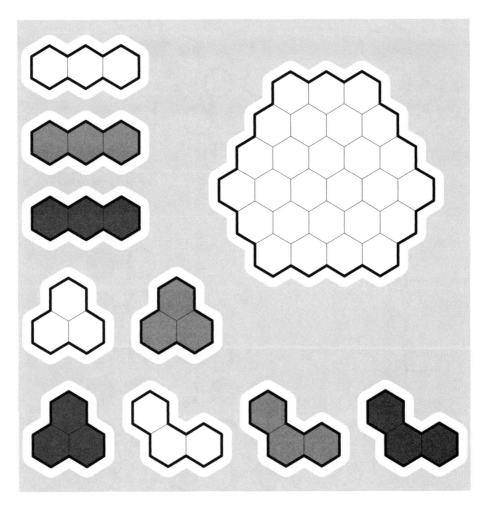

Place all of the pieces consisting of three adjacent hexagons into the grid shown above right. Pieces of the same color must not touch each other.

The New Puzzle Classics

The Tri-Hex Puzzle

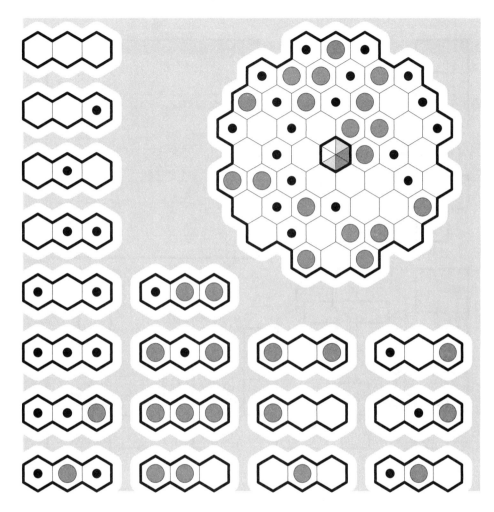

The grid with the pattern shown above at right was formed from the eighteen pieces scattered next to it. How was it done? Draw the lines between the pieces on the grid. All eighteen pieces must be used. You may rotate the pieces as you wish, but you may not overlap them.

Distorted Pentashapes

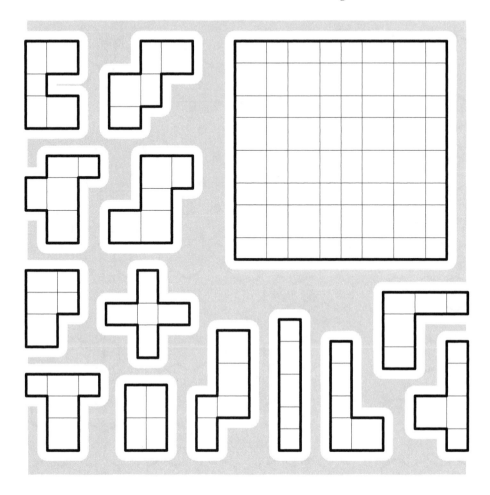

The square grid shown above right can be made with the thirteen pieces scattered next to it. How can all the pieces be placed within the grid? Draw the lines between them. The outlines of the pieces (and the lines on them) must exactly match the lines in the grid. You may rotate the pieces as you want, but you may neither turn them over nor overlap them.

The Nine Bat-Squares

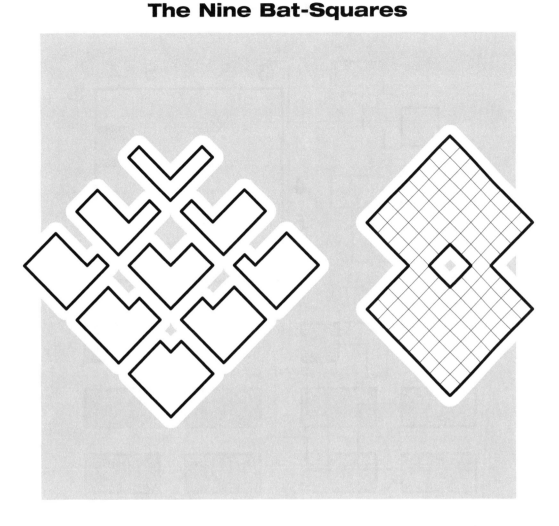

Place all the nine bat-squares shown in the left illustration into the 8-like shape on the right. The pieces may be rotated, but neither overlapped nor turned over.

Touch-Me-Not Blocks

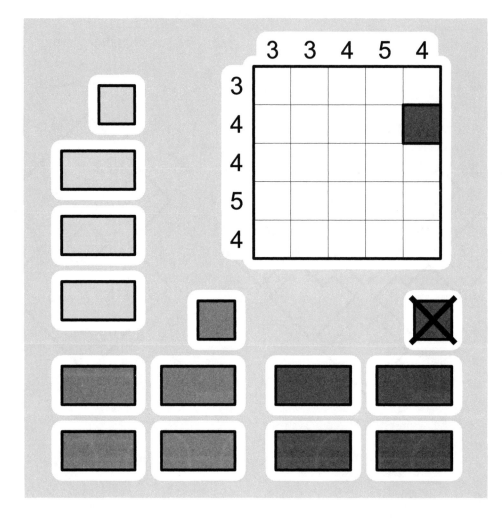

Into the 5 X 5 square (above right), place all fourteen pieces scattered next to it so that no two pieces of the same color touch each other, even diagonally. The numbers next to each row and column of the square show how many pieces (or their parts) can be found in that respective row or column. You may rotate the pieces, but you may not overlap them. One piece is already shown in the right position.

Checkered Dominoes

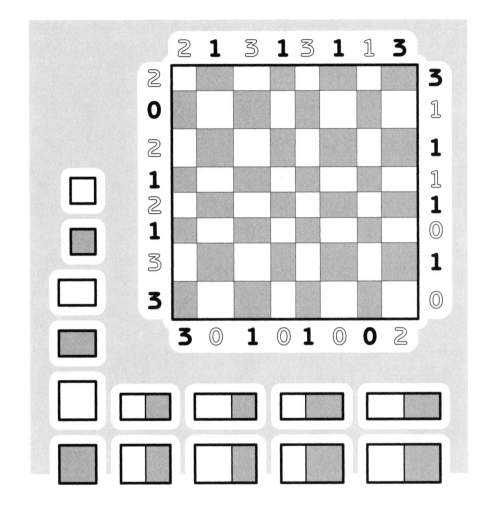

Place the fourteen pieces—six monominoes and eight dominoes shown next to the square diagram in the upper right—in this diagram so that the following are true:

1. The outlines of each piece exactly match the lines of the diagram.

2. The color(s) of each piece match the color(s) of the respective cell(s) of the diagram—white with white, and shaded with shaded.

3. Every piece is be oriented either horizontally or vertically.

4. No two pieces touch each other, even diagonally.

The light and dark digits around the diagram show how many cells of the diagram in the corresponding lines (rows or columns) are occupied by pieces and/or their parts. The light digits show the number of white cells and the dark digits show the number of shaded cells, respectively. The digits at each line do not show how white and shaded elements are placed in the line; their order is not shown.

The Puzzle Park

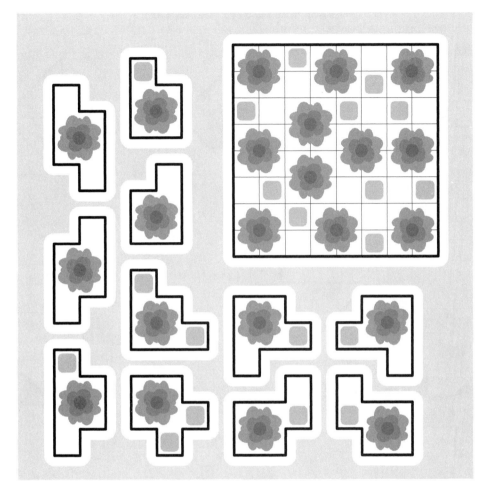

The Central Puzzle Park shown in the upper right illustration is divided into eleven grounds, each of which contains a tree. These grounds are shown just next to the park. Can you find out how all these grounds are situated within the park? You may rotate pieces as you wish, but you may neither overlap nor turn them over.

The Checkered Tangram: Dog, Fox, Goose & Corn

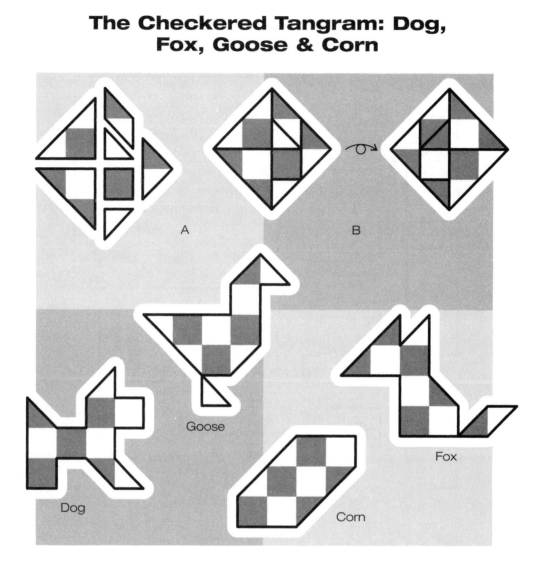

This puzzle is based on the traditional tangram puzzle consisting of seven pieces, but with two substantial differences. First, it is checkered. Second, its pieces are two-sided with contrast colors in every pair of single cells on their opposite sides. These new features present the tangram in a new puzzling form. Illustration A (uppermost left) shows all seven pieces of the checkered tangram. Illustration B shows both sides of the square assembled from the seven checkered pieces.

The object of the challenge called "Dog, Fox, Goose & Corn" is to show how each of the four shapes below the squares can be assembled using all seven pieces. You may rotate the pieces and flip them over, but overlapping is not permitted. Remember that the patterns on the opposite sides of every piece are exact opposites.

Last but not least, here is one more variation on famous river-crossing puzzles, which have been very popular (and yet, surprisingly, very rare) for many centuries. Using a small boat, a farmer has to cross a river and take his dog, goose, corn, and fox. The boat may only carry the farmer and either his dog, goose, corn, or fox. The fox cannot be left alone (without the farmer's presence) with the dog and/or the goose. The goose can be left with the corn just in case, *if* the dog is left, which will watch over the corn, but will not eat the goose. Can you help the farmer solve this challenge?

Wrap the Box

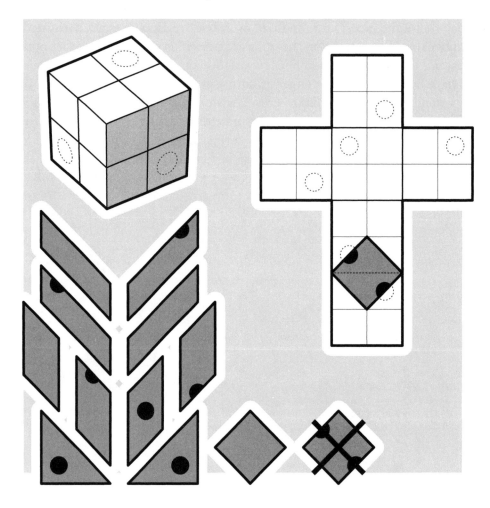

Using the twelve pieces shown above, wrap the 2 X 2 X 2 cube (see the uppermost left illustration). In wrapping the box, you may fold the pieces as you wish, but you may neither overlap nor flip them over. You should have the cube fully wrapped, with six whole spots (exactly one spot per side) on its surface as shown on its layout on the right. The layout is provided to solve the puzzle; just draw the pieces on it. As a hint, one piece is already shown in its correct position.

The Color Grains Puzzle

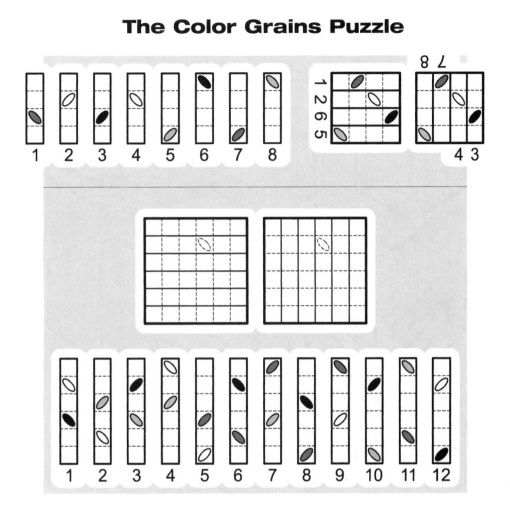

Place all twelve strips (numbered 1 through 12 just above) to form the two squares shown just over them so that the following are true:

1. Six strips lie within the left square horizontally, and the other six strips lie within the right square vertically.

2. Color grains in both squares form an identical pattern, including a color, place, and orientation for each grain. In other words, if you place one square onto another in the orientation as they are shown (with no turning), then each grain from one square must exactly match the same color grain in another square.

3. You may turn strips, but you are not allowed to turn them over or overlap them. The position of one grain is already shown in each square.

The uppermost illustration shows a small example with eight strips that illustrates the above rules.

The Hexa-Spiral Path Puzzle

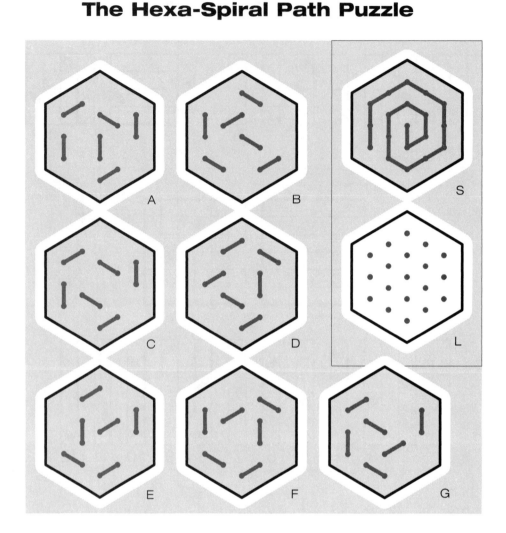

Each of the seven transparent hexagons (A–G) above has six fragments of some path depicted on it. Which three (and only three) from these can form the Hexa-Spiral Path—exactly as that shown in diagram S—when they are stacked up in a pile? You may rotate the hexagons and flip them over. The lattice in diagram L is provided for your convenience while you solve the puzzle and draw fragments of the path.

Interlocked Rings

The four patterns above (A, B, C, and D) are assembled from four interwoven paper rings each. In just one pattern, all of its rings are interlocked and thus cannot be separated into single rings without breaking some of them. One of the other patterns consists of an inseparable group of three rings, plus one separate one. Another pattern is composed of two linked and two separate rings. And, finally, there is a pattern assembled of four fully separate rings. Note that every ring in all of the groups forms a closed loop. To make an inseparable group of rings in some patterns, respective (locking) rings were cut, and after they were interwoven with some other ones, these locking rings were patched, so that they were restored to unbroken closed rings as they were before they were cut.

Can you find out which inseparable group of rings and/or separate rings make up every pattern, and which rings make up every inseparable group? To show the solution, refer to the letters next to every pattern.

Quadrangles

How many quadrangles of all shapes and sizes can you find in this pattern? Quadrangles may be both convex and concave. As a warm-up, you may count all possible triangles of all possible sizes first. Note that in both puzzles, shapes that are mirror images of each other are counted separately.

How Many Candies?

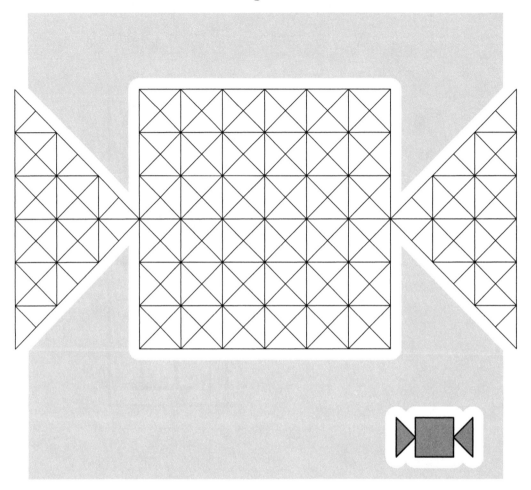

How many candies of all possible sizes can you find within the large grid above? All candies must be similar in shape to that shown in the small illustration beneath the grid.

The Time Pictoscope

The symbols displayed in the screens of the time pictoscope represent ancient cultural attributes. The challenge is to discover the ninth symbol, which is still missing. Can you reveal this ancient enigma?

The Field of Hearts Challenge

Only one heart from among all the hearts covering the field of hearts has its twin—an exactly identical heart also located in the field. Can you find this pair of loving hearts? Note that they *cannot* be mirror images of each other.

Chapter **5**

WORDS & NUMBERS

Puzzles with words and numbers form a large part of the repertoire of the Puzzle World, and are popular in every country. Over the centuries, it has become more difficult to discover new and never-before-seen puzzles in this field. Still, there are infinite possibilities as to how to play with words and numbers, and numerous ways to create new and pleasant challenges.

This chapter presents a collection of puzzles that play with letters, words, digits, and numbers in both traditional and nontraditional ways. Again, the visual element is emphasized, forming the majority of puzzles gathered in this chapter. They play with numerous facets of words and numbers, including their visual properties and internal senses, values, and unexpected properties. As a result, these challenges are unusual and funny, stimulate the imagination, and foster solving skills.

Themes in this chapter include common words and sentences, math sequences and equations, word and number patterns (as those presented in the previous chapter), arithmetical and word rebuses (including some performed with matchsticks), and word and number dissections and transformations.

There are no special formulas to solve the puzzles presented in this chapter, so in most cases you will have to try your own approaches to solve these challenges. You will need some general knowledge, common sense, and a good deal of observation and logical reasoning.

Test-Fest

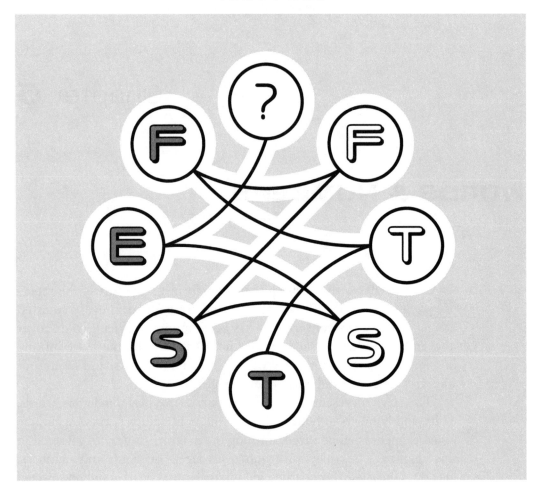

Which letter should be placed in the circle with the question mark? *Note:* The solution is not E!

The O-O-O-O Puzzle

Which letter do you think should be placed in the top box instead of the question mark?

The Word Tower

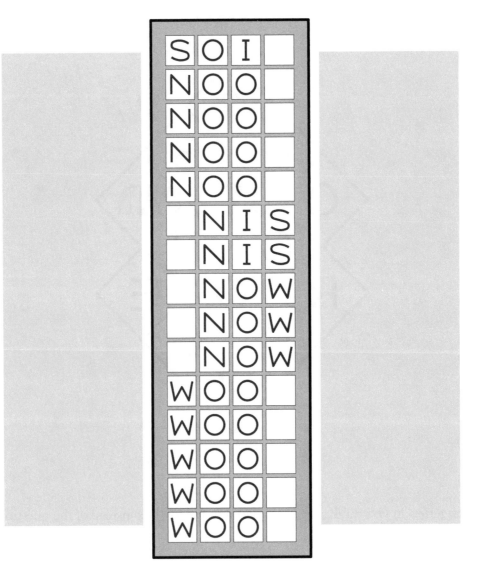

Fill in all the empty windows in the word tower shown above (one letter per window) to form fifteen complete words. How long will it take you to perform this?

The New Puzzle Classics

The Letter Weeding

The words in each of the four lines presented above consist of letters chosen in accordance with one basic rule. For every line, the rules are similar. Can you discover their general principle? As a hint, neither increasing the number of the letters in the words within each line, nor the presence of some letters repeating within the first three, is part of the correct answer.

Letter Quest

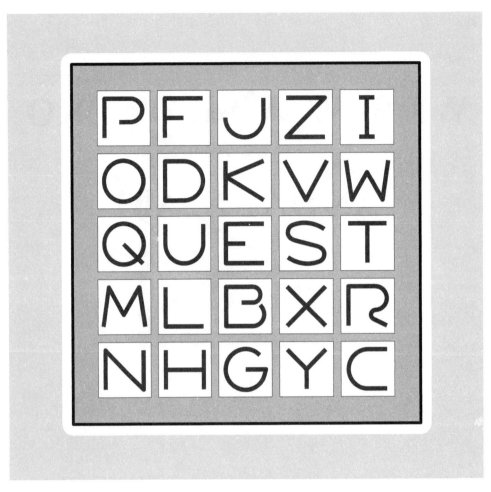

All the letters of the English alphabet except one (A) were distributed within a 5 X 5 square according to a basic rule. Then, two pairs of adjacent letters were chosen, and the letters within every pair were swapped. The resulting 5 X 5 square is shown above. Can you discover the rule that was applied to the distribution of letters within the initial 5 X 5 square, and which four letters should now be swapped in pairs so that the square will be restored to its original position to fully satisfy that rule?

The New Puzzle Classics

The Quick Puzzle

What does the picture shown above mean?

The Foxy Box

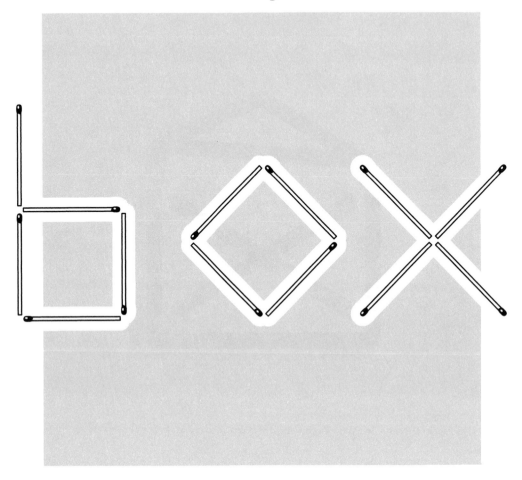

Move exactly one matchstick to change the "box" into an animal. You may not use a mirror.

Mice & Cat

The word "mice" is assembled above from five parts. Can you reassemble them so that they read "cat"? You may rotate the pieces, but no overlapping is permitted. Keep in mind that all the letters of "cat" must be of the same height, must be placed in a straight line, and must not touch each other, even at a corner.

One Square

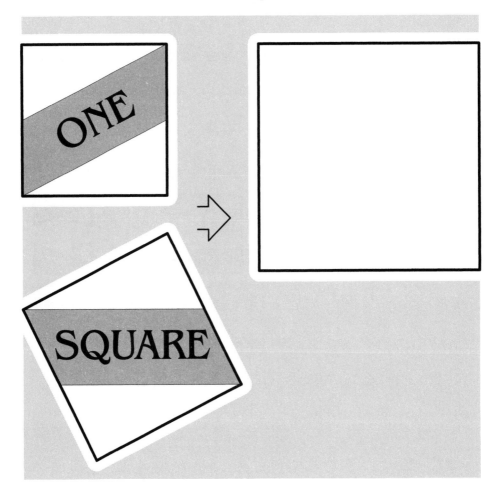

Divide the two smaller squares on the left (those containing the words "one" and "square") into five parts, and assemble them into the big square shown on the right. You may not cut the shaded parts of the squares, nor are you allowed to overlap the pieces or flip them over.

The New Puzzle Classics

Moon & Star

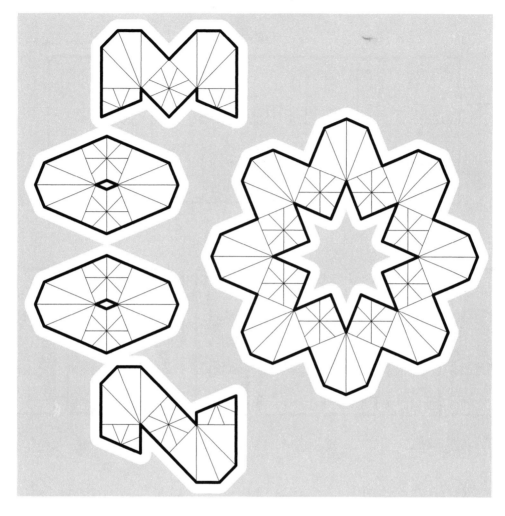

Divide the four letters in "moon" at left into the minimum number of pieces (but no more than three parts per letter) to rearrange them into the star shown on the right. You may rotate pieces, but you may not flip them over or overlap them.

The Challenge of the Wall Maze

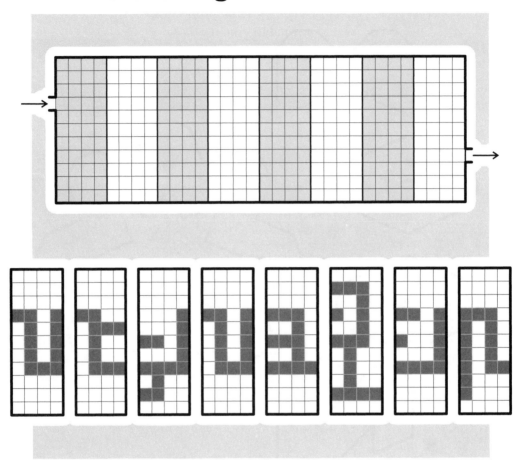

An archaeological expedition discovered a hidden room in the Palace of the Sun Rain with eight wall panels with fragments of a maze lying on the floor at an empty wall. An ancient architect left his work unfinished as a message to future generations. Can you reveal the mystery of the wall maze and read the message?

The wall and all eight panels are shown in the illustrations above. As it is shown in the illustration, the maze should have only one entrance and one exit, as shown by the two arrows. These are the only two points where the maze connects to the periphery of the wall. The maze takes a narrow, continuous path from the entrance to the exit, and has several narrow dead-end paths. "Narrow" means that there is no place within the maze where its pattern makes an area measuring 2 X 2 or larger.

No parts of the maze diagonally self-touch at any point. All fragments of the maze must form an uninterrupted path.

Panels may be turned upside-down, but you may not overlap or flip them over. The vertical shaded parts on the wall are provided for your convenience while solving. *Hint:* After you restore the maze, it will show a *single* word (formed from *all* the paths of the maze) that describes the sense of this ancient challenge.

Hard As XYZ

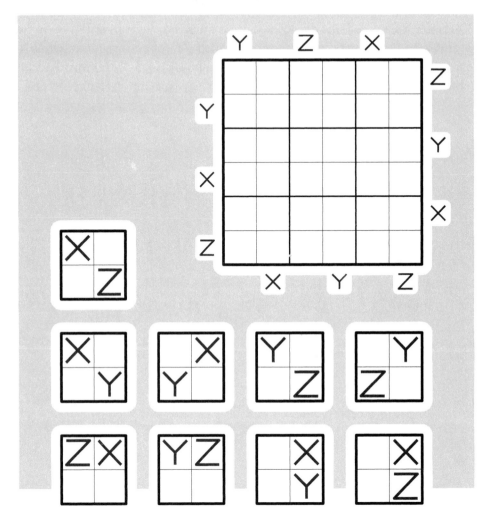

Place all nine small pieces with the letters on them shown above within the 6 X 6 grid at the top right so that each of its rows and columns contains exactly three letters—X, Y, and Z, not necessarily in that order. The small letters around the outside of the grid will help you to determine the order of the letters within each letter triplet and the cells they will occupy. The letters in each triplet need not all be adjacent to each other. The presence of a small outside letter means that it can not be seen from that direction (from that point) as the first letter in the letter triplet in the respective row/column. *Hint:* Note that no two cells with the same letter may touch each other, even diagonally. Some pieces can be rotated 180 degrees, but only those with depicted X or Z, since after rotation they will look exactly as in their original orientation. You may not turn over and/or overlap the pieces.

If & Then

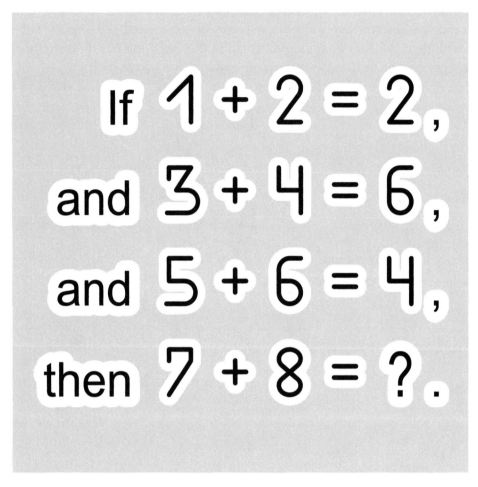

If $1 + 2 = 2$,

and $3 + 4 = 6$,

and $5 + 6 = 4$,

then $7 + 8 = ?$.

The four equations interwoven within the sentence above are based on some hidden sense and rule. The challenge is to find out which number can replace the question mark. *Hint:* Both the value and shape of the numbers are important in solving the puzzle.

Puzzler's Merry-Go-Round

Starting from the "1" on the above clockface and going clockwise, write out all its digits in the following line: 1 2 3 4 5 6 7 8 9 1 0 1 1 1 2. The object of this puzzle is to insert some of the four arithmetical signs ("+", "-", "X", and "÷") so that the sum of the equation is 365. You may use any number of the signs in any combination (even several times for some of them) and order in the final solution, but you may not change the order of the digits in the line. As an example, the following expression shows how the sum of 328 can be obtained from the row of these digits: 12 ÷ 3 + 45 + 67 + 8 + 91 + 0 + 111 + 2 = 328.

4 - 3 =

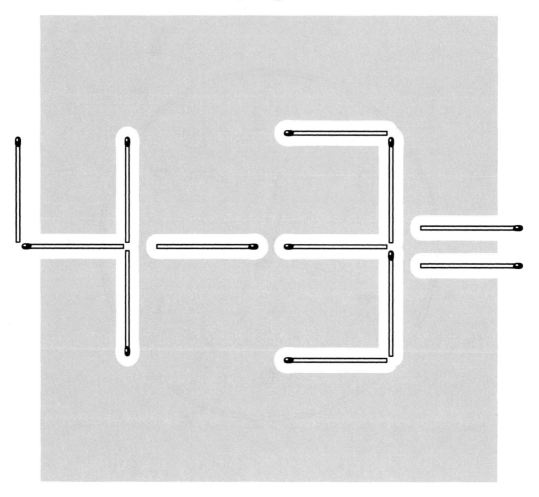

Move three matchsticks to form a correct equation.

The New Puzzle Classics

The Puzzle of the "VII"

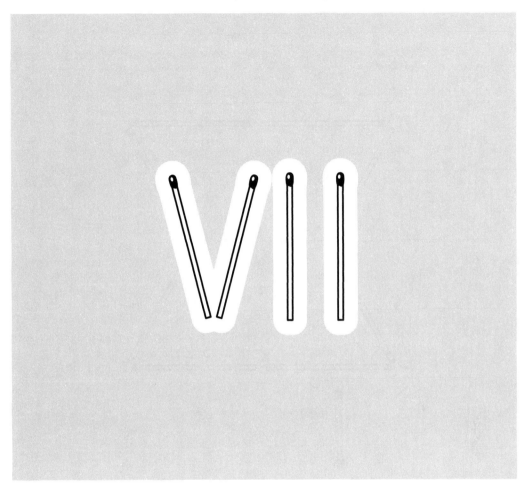

Move two matchsticks to change this seven into four tens. Matchsticks may overlap.

The X-Symmetry Challenge

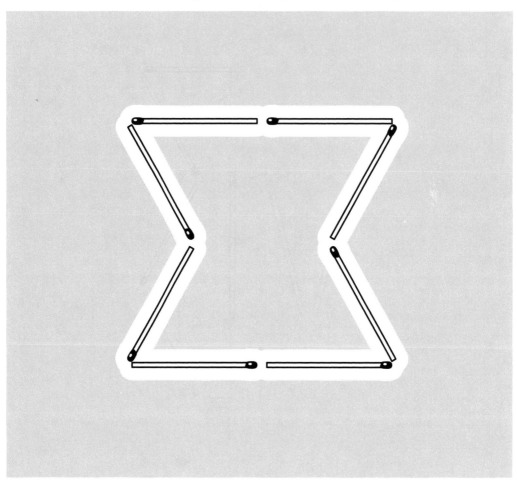

Move exactly three matchsticks to change the symmetric Roman ten shown above into a symmetric Roman five.

The New Puzzle Classics

Hexa Six

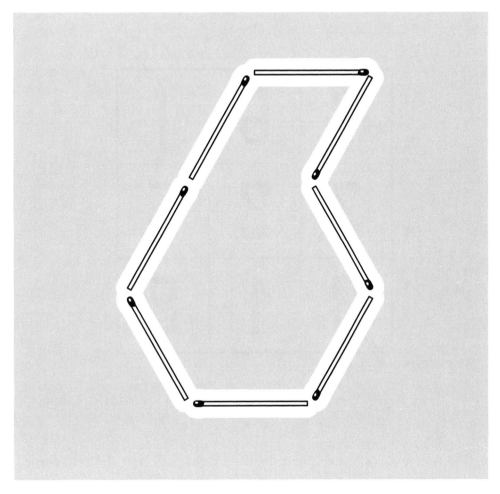

Divide the six-like shape shown above with four matchsticks into:

1. Two parts of the same area.

2. Three parts of the same area.

3. Four parts of the same area and shape.

Magic 3 X 3 Dissection

The 3 X 3 square above contains nine digits—1 through 9. Your task is to divide the square into three parts differing in area and/or shape, so that they can be rearranged into a traditional 3 X 3 magic square with the magic sum 15. This means that every row, column, and each of the two main diagonals will add up to 15. This puzzle can be solved in two different ways, each with three different pieces. Can you discover both solutions?

The Eight-Into-Zero Change

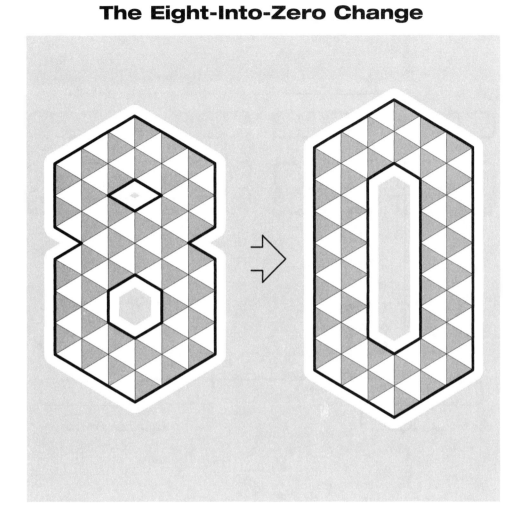

Divide the checkered eight shown on the left into four pieces—*different* and *noncongruent* (see the introduction to Chapter 1)—so that they can be rearranged into the checkered zero shown on the right. You may rotate pieces, but you may neither overlap nor flip them over. Note that the checkered pattern of the zero must be exactly as shown. After you crack this puzzle, try to solve a somewhat opposite challenge and discover how to divide the zero shape into only two *congruent* pieces so that they can be rearranged into *another* symmetrical, regularly checkered eight.

The Zero-Infinity Mystery

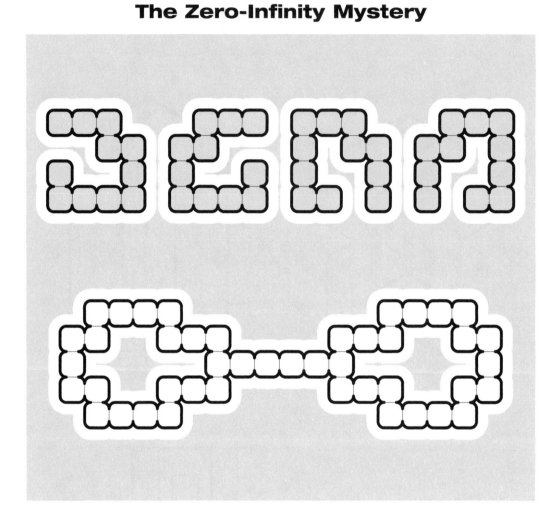

A time machine, from its journey through the future, has sent—among many other images—one which is shown above. The message reads:

". . . Just into eight parts zero breaks—that is the way it infinity makes . . . "

Now, the challenge is to discover how to divide the four letters of the word "zero" into eight pieces so that they will make the infinity sign depicted beneath it. Can you do it?

Invisible Digital Tiling

All ten digits above—1 through 0—are hidden within the grid shown in the upper-most diagram. Can you find them all? The digits may touch each other and rotate, but may not overlap and/or flip over. Their outlines (including the internal lines depicted on them) must coincide exactly with the lines in the grid. Note that every digit is formed of three exactly equal P-shaped elements. These elements are called hexaminoes, since each of them consists of six small unit squares.

The Wire Count

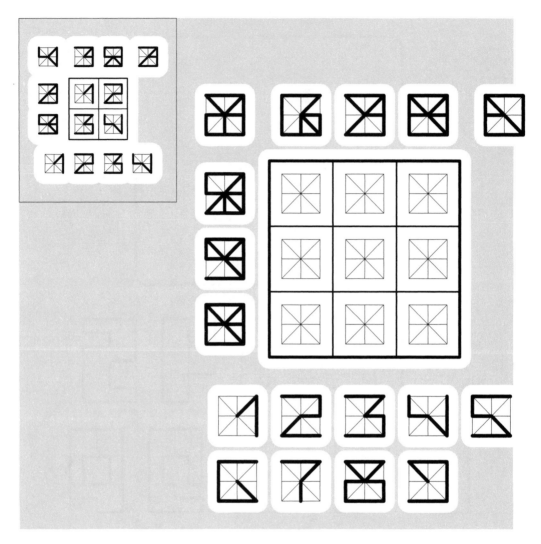

In the 3 X 3 diagram above (center right), place all nine digits shown below it—one digit per square—so that when you stack three digits from a row, column, or diagonal, you will obtain the pattern shown just next to (above or at left) the corresponding row, column, or each of the two main diagonals, respectively. You may neither rotate nor turn over the digits. The uppermost left illustration shows a small four-digit example with its solution.

The Reed Number Maze

The uppermost illustration shows several reed numbers placed within a simple spiral maze. The numbers appear according to a certain rule, but one of them is omitted. Which number from among those shown in the bottom line (1 through 0) should replace the question mark within the maze?

Chapter 6

ORIGAMI PUZZLES

The most unusual thing about origami puzzles is that a very small number of examples of this very rare type of puzzles have been created to date. Despite the fact that the art of origami has been well known for several thousand years and is now very popular all over the world, origami puzzles are relatively new. Origami puzzles are part of the larger category of folding puzzles, yet they are so distinctive that they form an amazing and almost independent field with its own rules and properties.

Generally, the object in origami puzzles is to fold a piece of paper several times in order to form some predetermined shape with a special pattern or specific properties. The first rule in classic origami (and, thus, for the origami puzzles collected in this chapter) is that you begin with a square piece of paper (or several pieces equal in size for some puzzles) colored on one of its sides and white on the other; this is a traditional ("standard") paper shape for most origami creations. I call such a square an "origami square." The second rule is that you are allowed only to fold an origami square; you may not cut and paste. All but three of the puzzles in this chapter strictly obey these main rules. The three "nonstandard" origami puzzles are included to illustrate how other types of puzzles can be created using standard origami squares.

The first part of this chapter contains origami puzzles with specified patterns on their face sides only, and some with two-sided patterns, including three two-sided nonstandard origami puzzles. In the second part of this chapter, about a dozen novel origami puzzles with two-sided "contrast" shapes are presented. Both sides of these shapes have exactly the same patterns, but their colors are the exact *opposite* on the face and back. You will recognize these puzzles from special double diagrams showing the front and back of the final patterns; the front side of the final shape is always shown on the left, with the back one on the right. This symbol ↺ means that the shape is flipped around its vertical axis.

For all the origami puzzles presented in this chapter, there are some additional specific rules:

1. You are allowed to make simple folds (sometimes called "book folds") without any special twists. Such a fold assumes that we fold one or several layers of paper simultaneously, and the fold is counted as a single fold.

2. All puzzles presented in this chapter are flat—their final shapes must be flat. At the same time, shapes may have several layers of paper at any point.

3. When we see plain color elements of some pattern to create in its final form, in fact, it may be not only a plain color surface, but also a combined one-colored area consisting of several one-colored parts that may touch one another along some line, or even overlap. The same is true for white elements in final patterns.

4. Mutual sizes of different shapes proposed as origami challenges are relative, and depend on the actual sizes of the origami squares you use for each of them. For instance, if you use an origami square of the same size for every puzzle, the sizes of different final shapes will vary from those presented in the chapter. One useful suggestion is that if you have origami squares of several different sizes, it may be more convenient to use larger origami squares for origami challenges with a greater number of requested folds, and, similarly, smaller origami squares for challenges with fewer folds.

5. There are different methods (for example, Haga theorems) developed to create special angles such as 15, 30, or 60 degrees, or to divide a side of an origami square into 2, 3, 4, or 5 parts just by folding the square, without any additional tools. For the purpose of solving origami puzzles these methods may be very useful, but if you use additional tools (such as a ruler, triangle, or pencil) to mark the lines or angles on your origami square, this is also acceptable.

6. If you need to precrease your origami square to find the correct lines and points for future folds, you may do this as needed, but before you start to fold the goal shape, you should fully unfold your origami square to get it flat, and after that you may start to count your final folds. And, please, remember that only book folds are allowed!

7. A final remark: It is more convenient to use several origami squares when you solve a puzzle; one is for the first-draft folds, the next ones are to finalize the solution.

Fold Two to Three

Take two origami squares, fold each of them just once, and then put them together so that you can see three squares. How can it be done? Note that you may not overlap the pieces.

Three-Into-One Folds

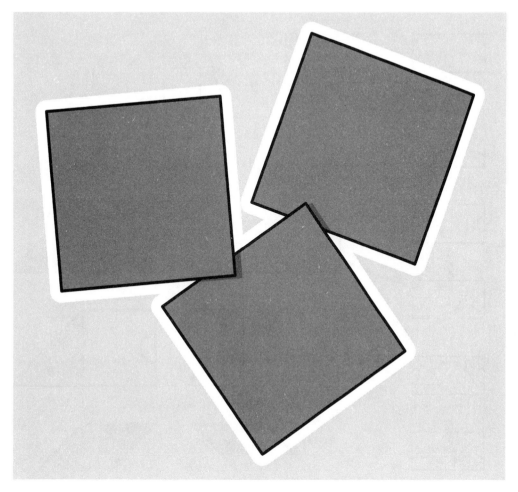

Fold each of these three origami squares no more than two times each to form three shapes that can form a perfect, fully colored square of the maximal area. These shapes must be fully colored on both of their sides. You may not overlap the shapes in the final square.

The Origami Mini-Dominoes

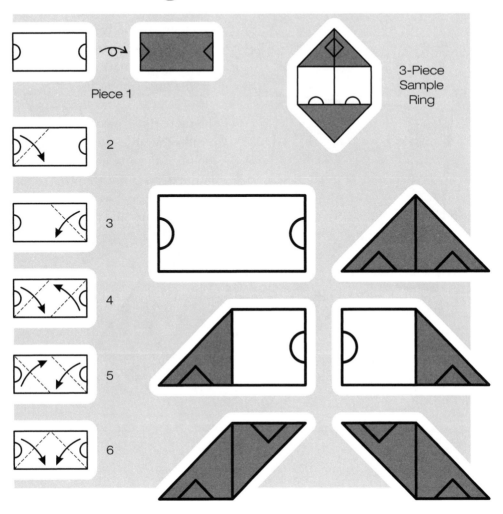

Divide an origami square into eight small rectangular pieces with the proportions of their sides 1:2 to obtain eight paper dominoes. Discard two of them, and mark the remaining six with two marks on each side as shown in the uppermost left double diagram. One of them will be Piece 1. Then fold the remaining five as shown in diagrams 2 through 6 on the left. Use a drop of glue to fix their flaps. The final set of the origami mini-dominoes is shown in the bottom right illustration.

The object of this puzzle is to assemble a continuous, closed paper ribbon colored on one side and white on the other, by placing dominoes one after another so that the color of their sides and marks will match exactly on both of its sides. As a result, going along the ribbon you should see on its colored side a chain of small squares, and on its white side a chain of small circles. Every mark must be paired up with its twin, and no lost marks must be found in the final ribbon.

You should keep in mind that the ribbon is two-layered, so sometimes a domino is joined to the bottom layer of its neighbor. The small three-piece sample of such a ribbon, shown in the uppermost right diagram, will show an example of all connections in the ribbon. Your ribbon, in fact, is a loop (or ring), and may have any shape. It may touch itself at any point or line (just as in the three-piece sample). You may flip pieces over, but you may not overlap them.

It is also possible to assemble similar ribbons using four- and five-piece subsets chosen from the whole set. As a warm-up, you may try these simpler challenges before you start to play with the whole six-piece set.

Three-Strip-Triangle

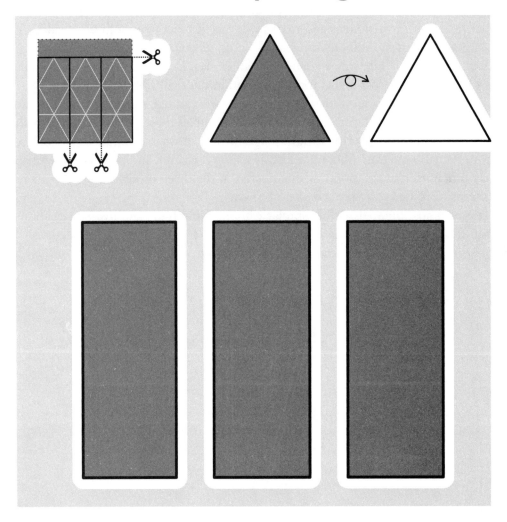

The three strips above are cut from an origami square as shown in the uppermost left diagram. Repeat two single folds for each strip to form three shapes that can then be interwoven to form an equilateral triangle fully colored on its face side and white on its back, as shown in the uppermost right double diagram.

The New Puzzle Classics

The Woven Colored Square

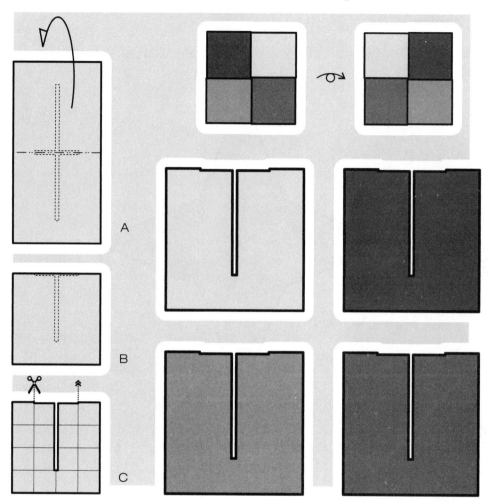

This puzzle consists of four rectangles in four different colors. Every rectangle is half of an origami square. For this puzzle, you need to perform a crosslike cut along the dotted line within each rectangle as shown in diagram A. The easy way to do this is to fold a rectangle in half (diagram B), and then make a T-shaped cut with scissors as shown in diagram C. The puzzle pieces are shown on the right as four colored squares. Now interweave all these squares into a flat square packet with four colors on every side, exactly as shown in the uppermost right double diagram.

The Star of Origami

Take an origami square and, always going around its center, repeat each of three simple folds four times so that a star will appear as shown above. You may have some white parts around the star's outline. The back side of the final shape may have any pattern.

The Checkered Origami Trimino

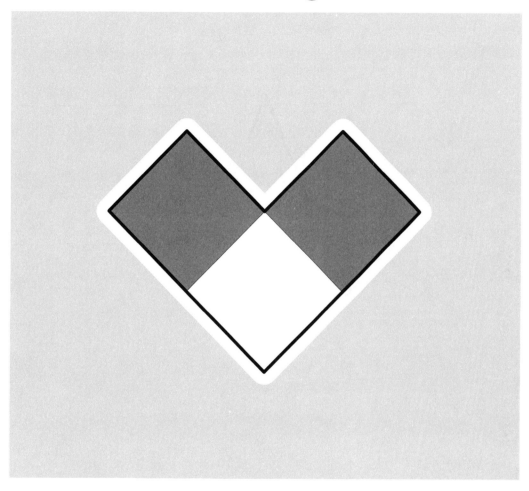

The above checkered trimino can be formed with four single folds of an origami square. Can you figure out how to do this? The back side of the final trimino may have any pattern.

Skew Trimino Pattern

Fold an origami square into the above striped trimino with only five single folds. The back side of the final shape may have any pattern.

The New Puzzle Classics

The Origami Checkerboard Puzzle

Fold an origami square several times to get a smaller square with the checkered pattern as shown in the above diagram. The back side of the final square may have any pattern. The first challenge is to do this with seven single folds. After you have done that, try to form the same pattern with six single folds. The last challenge is even more difficult. Can you form this pattern with only five single folds?

This origami checkerboard puzzle presents a basic challenge, which with the effort of many puzzle and origami folks has evolved and been widely popularized. Koji Kitajima and Hiroshi Yamamoto not only have found a minimal five-fold solution to the basic pattern, but together with Setsuo Sasaki also discovered many similar checkered patterns and found minimal solutions to them. Nob Yoshigahara, the largest creator of puzzles, made a presentation at the Gathering for Gardner 3 in Atlanta in 1998 of this challenge with additional patterns. Andy Liu made use of this puzzle in education with the activity called Scientific Origami; its basic part consists in making different checkered patterns using origami squares precreased into 4 X 4 and 5 X 5 grids. This puzzle has also appeared on the Web. Particularly, many of its patterns along with minimal necessary folds can be found at the OrigamiUSA Web site (www.origami-usa.org) presented by Tom Hull, and at the British Origami Society Web site (www.britishorigami.org.uk/fun/sasaki.htm).

There are fifty different two-colored patterns to the origami checkerboard puzzle. You can easily find any of these patterns. Just draw a 3 X 3 grid, and then blacken 1, 2, 3, or 4 of its cells as you wish in any position within the grid. Four cells are always enough, since even if you blacken 5, 6, 7, or 8 cells, you will have, in fact, the same patterns, but with mutually contrasting colors. In any case, the only challenge for you will be to find a minimum number of single folds to form the checkered pattern you have just generated.

The Origami Propeller

The square propeller shown above can be formed from an origami square. Keeping in mind its rotational symmetry, you can create this pattern by repeating each of four single folds exactly four times. Of course, you should discover these single folds first. Note that the back side of the propeller may have any pattern.

The Origami House Puzzle

Fold an origami square exactly six times to build the house shown above. Its shape contains one floor (a white 1 X 2 rectangle) and a colored roof (an equilateral triangle). The goal is to build the largest house possible. The house may have any pattern on its back.

The Origami Greek Cross

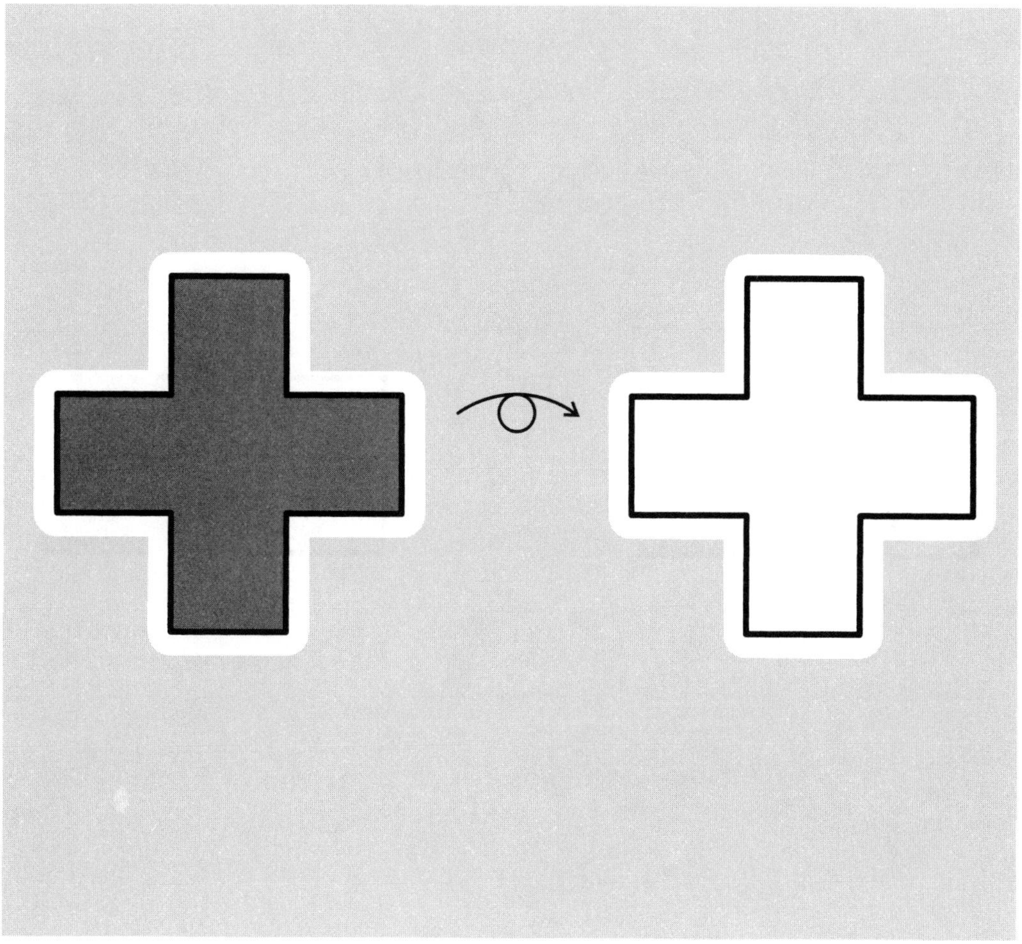

The Greek cross with the fully colored face side and the white back shown above can be folded from an origami square. For this challenge, because of its rotational symmetry, your goal is to find out only three basic folds, and then repeat each of them exactly four times, going around the center of the square all the time.

The Origami Domino

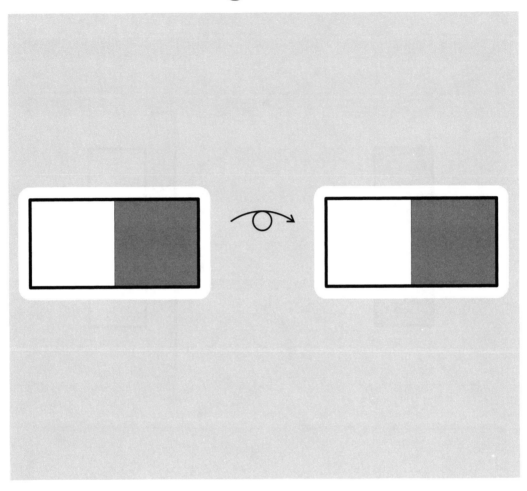

A simple origami domino. It can be formed from an origami square with only three single folds. How can it be done?

The Checkered Trimino

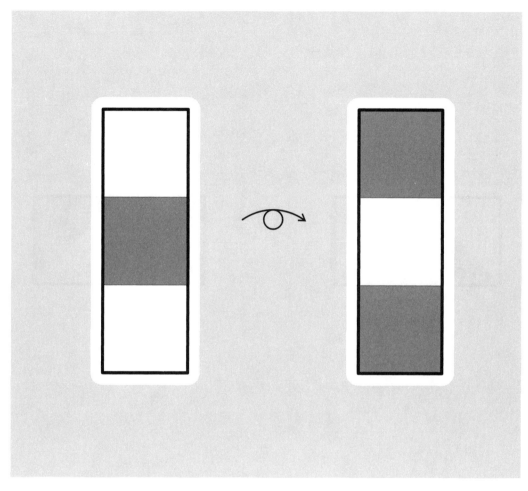

The above checkered trimino is two-sided. Can you form it from an origami square making six single folds?

Triangle-In-Rectangle

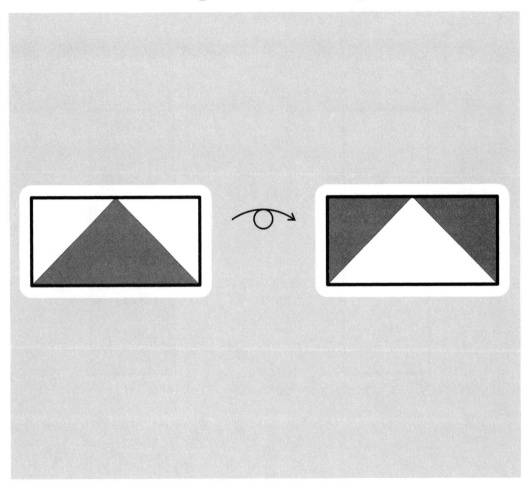

Can you find how to form the "triangle-in-rectangle" domino shown above by folding an origami square seven times?

Skew Domino Pattern

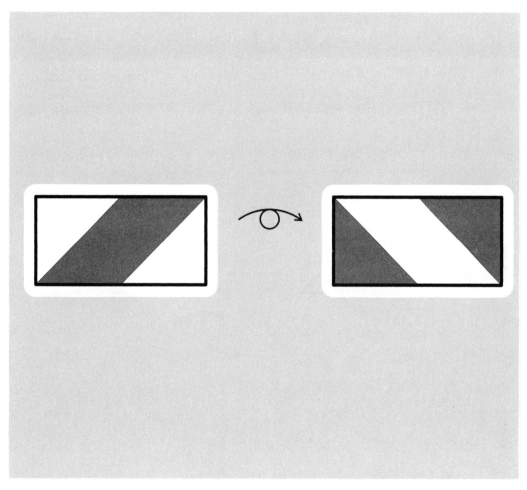

Fold an origami square ten times to get a rectangle with skew patterns on both sides as shown in the above diagrams. As challenging as a puzzle can be!

The Origami Hill

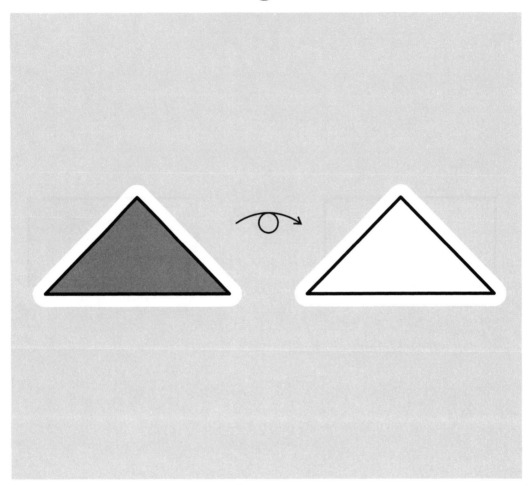

Fold an origami square only three times to get a triangle with the fully colored face side and the white back side as shown in the above diagrams.

Two Sides of the Mountain

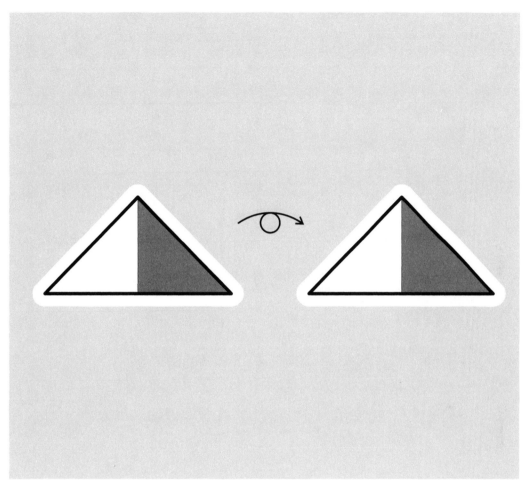

The above triangle can be folded with five single folds of an origami square. Your goal is to discover how it can be done.

The Mountain Seasons

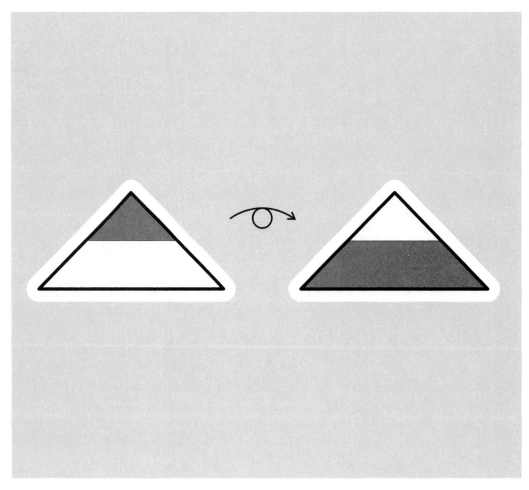

The higher we climb, the harder the challenges are! The mountain triangle shown above can be achieved with seven single folds of an origami square. Are you ready to conquer this puzzle peak?

The Checkered Mountain

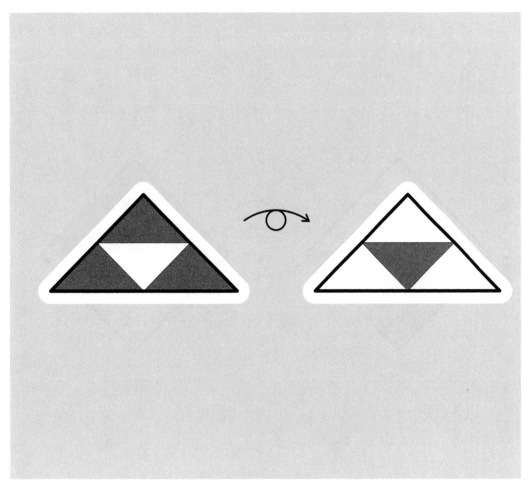

The above checkered triangle is one of the most challenging two-sided origami shapes. Can you fold an origami square into this triangle using nine single folds?

Lake & Mountain

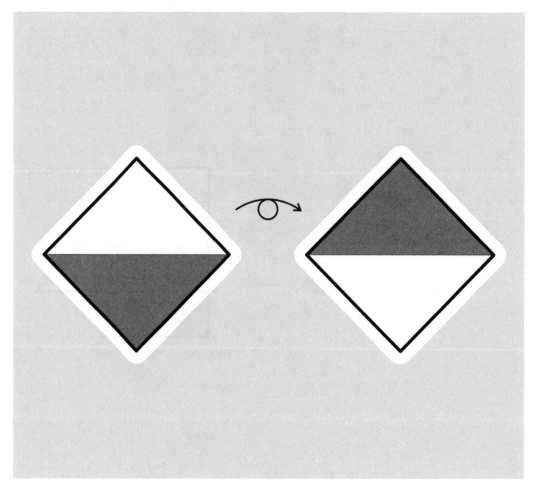

The square above can be folded from an origami square in five single folds. How can it be done?

The New Puzzle Classics

The Little Origami Chessboard

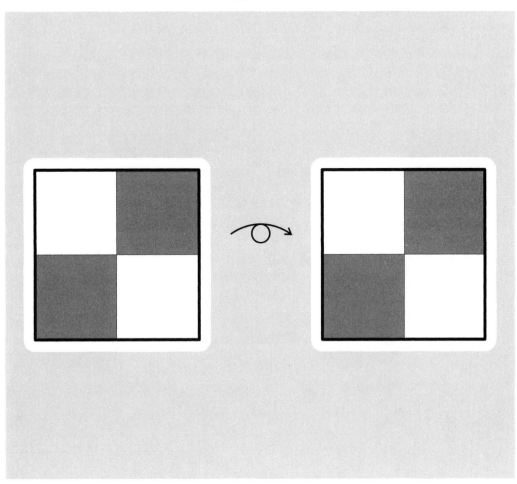

A puzzle for true chess and puzzle fans. To form the smallest possible two-sided chessboard, shown above, you will need an origami square and ten single folds. Can you win this game of origami chess?

Diagonal Crisscross

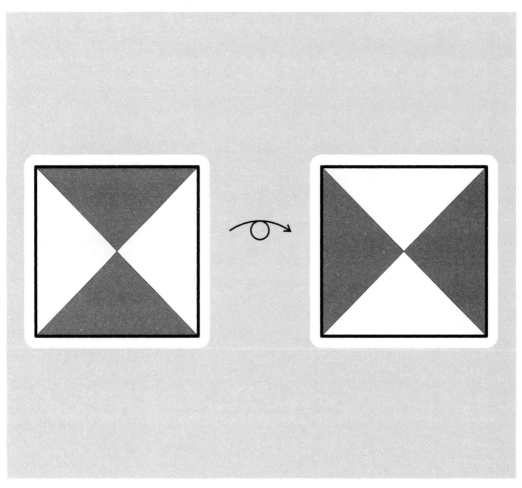

To fold an origami square into the diagonally checkered square shown above, you will need ten single folds. How can it be achieved?

The Origami Window

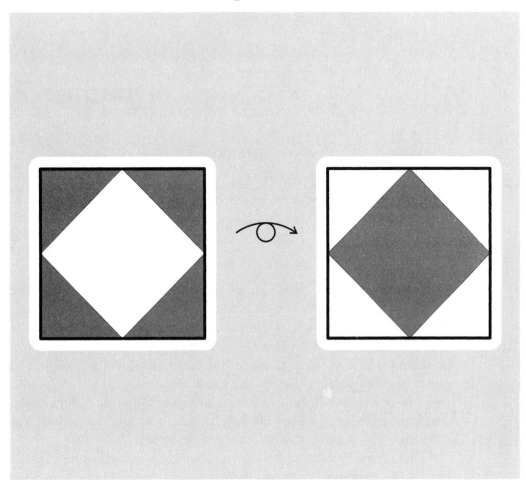

This very tricky pattern can really challenge you. The window above can be created from an origami square with twelve single folds. Good luck with this puzzle!

Chapter 7

TRICKY MOVES

Puzzles with moving pieces have always been very popular among puzzle lovers. A small collection of the newest challenges in this field is found in this chapter. To solve the puzzles collected here you will need just a few counters or coins. Every puzzle is presented with a big grid to place and move counters (or coins). The object of every puzzle is shown as a small double diagram, with its start position at left and its finish position at right. Different colors in the diagrams represent either different counters or different coins (or different sides—heads and tails—of the same coins).

This chapter consists of three parts. The first part contains six different puzzles of a traditional type with specially shaped boards. In these puzzles, counters move one at a time. The second part presents a dozen moving-piece puzzles of a totally new kind; these puzzles have twin-moves of their counters. The third and last part of the chapter is devoted to chess puzzles on special boards; instead of chess pieces you may use coins or similar objects.

Twin-move Puzzles

This type of newly developed moving-piece puzzle looks like traditional ones, but has specially designed boards (grids) allowing special twin-moves of counters. To perform a twin-move, you simply choose any pair of neighboring counters placed on the white spots connected with a *single* line (no matter of what color or colors the counters in every pair are), put two of your fingers on them, and then move this pair along the lines of the grid in one direction from one pair of small white spots to another. Note that you may not rotate the counter pair while moving it. You may move the same pair of counters in some further direction if there are free lines connecting this and some subsequent pair of white spots, *and* if there are no other counters in the way. Or you may choose another pair of neighboring counters, and move them.

It is obvious that the counters in such a pair must start and finish simultaneously, and may move along two parallel lines of the grid (sometimes these lines may partially coincide and form one long straight line). Every counter may be moved from just one small white spot to another, and cannot have intermediary stops on the line of the grid.

Some general rules for the puzzles in this chapter are as follows:

1. For all puzzles except chess challenges, your counters should perform only sliding moves. This means that you must move them on the board from cell to cell (from spot to spot) by only sliding them, without lifting. Thus, no jumps over any pieces are allowed. In the chess puzzles, you may both slide pieces or move them as in a normal chess play—lifting them from the board and then placing them on a free cell, but without jumping over any other pieces, except for the knight, which may jump over any piece.

2. In puzzles with square or hexagonal cells you may perform your moves between a pair of adjacent cells. For all chess puzzles in this chapter you should apply standard chess rules for moving chess pieces. In the grids consisting of small circular spots connected with lines, such as a spider's web, you should slide your pieces from spot to spot only along these grids' lines.

3. You may move a piece from cell to cell as long as it may move freely while observing the internal walls on some of them (represented with bold lines); you may not cross over them.

4. Placing pieces one on top of another is not allowed.

5. An uninterrupted move of a counter or pair of counters (in the case of twin-moves), or any chess piece (including a pawn) from its start cell to its end is counted as one move, no matter how long or curved the move is. The number of moves shown in the instructions to the puzzles are minimal, but you may set up your goal to solve every puzzle as close to these numbers as you wish.

Change the Levels

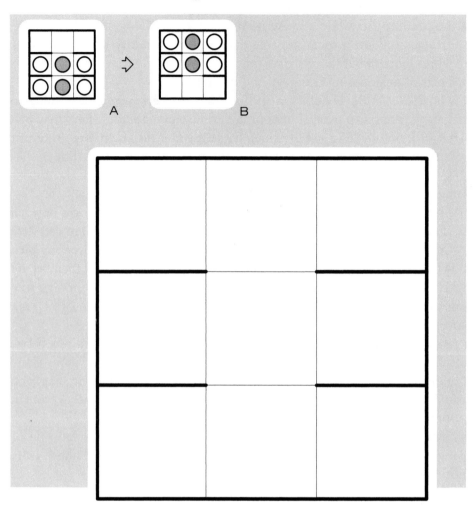

A   B

Place six counters or coins on the above 3 X 3 grid as shown in diagram A.
The object of the puzzle is to move counters to the pattern shown in diagram B
in nine single sliding moves.

Moves in the H

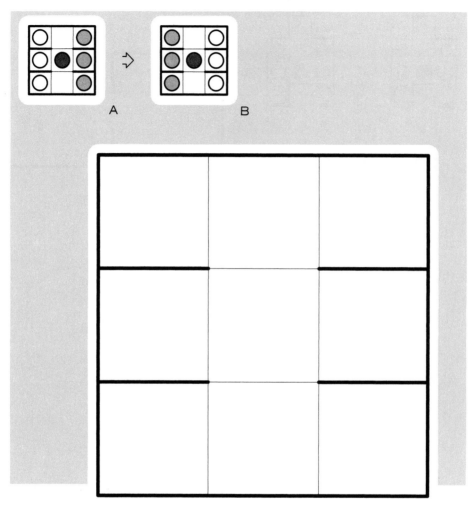

A   B

Place seven counters or coins of three different colors on the above 3 X 3 grid as shown in diagram A. The object of the puzzle is to form the H-pattern shown in diagram B in twelve single sliding moves.

Change the Columns

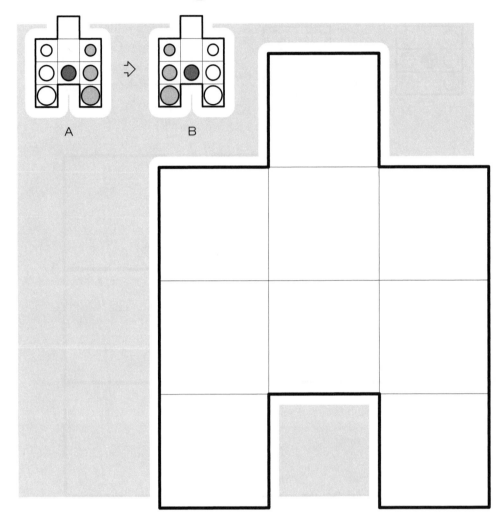

A   B

Seven counters or coins of three different colors and sizes placed on the above board form two columns with a bridge between them as shown in diagram A. By sliding one counter at a time, change the columns as shown in diagram A to those shown in diagram B in twenty-three single sliding moves. The middle counter must return to its starting place.

While moving counters you may not place any larger counters (regardless of color) in a column on the board over smaller counters, even if you move a counter across a column under a bigger one without stopping directly under it. Counters of the same size may move freely and be placed over one another. Generally speaking, different-sized counters in every column must always decrease going from bottom to top. If we mark the sizes of the counters as Big (B), Middle (M), and Small (S), legal positions, for example, may be as follows, going from bottom to top: B-M-S, B-M-M, B-S-S, M-M-M, M-M-S, M-S-S, B-M, B-S, M-S, and so on.

The Spiral Galaxy Mystery

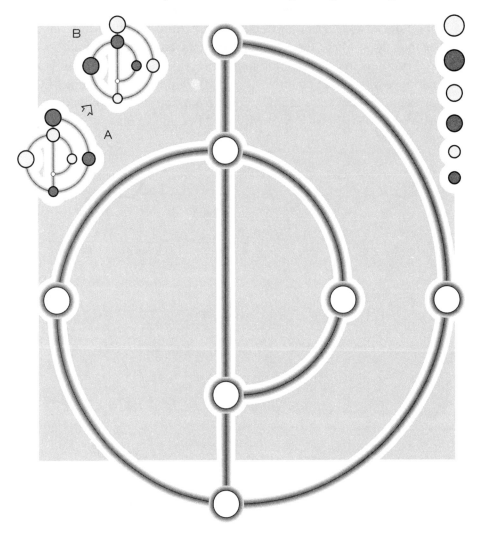

The stars that form this unique spiral galaxy shown above are Supernova, Nebula, Red Giant, Protostar, White Dwarf, and Black Dwarf. They are shown in the top right diagram. Place six counters of three different sizes in two colors (or respective coins) representing these stars on the above spiral as shown in the left illustration A. Your star challenge is to move the stars to the position shown in illustration B sliding one counter at a time, in fifteen single sliding moves.

The New Puzzle Classics

Bees & Ladybugs

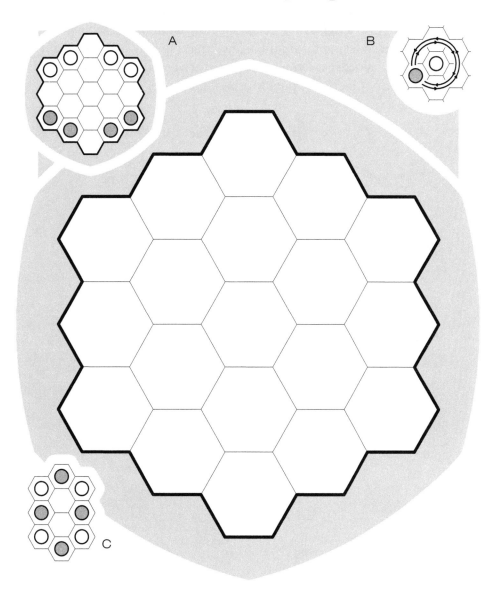

On the board, place eight counters or coins as shown in diagram A. The four shaded counters represent bees, while the four light ones are ladybugs. All pieces move over the board so that a chosen piece (bee or ladybug) always flies around one of its neighbors (bee or ladybug) only within the outline of the board, as shown in diagram B. No other moves (such as jumps or simple straight moves) are allowed.

Now flying with bees and ladybugs, rearrange them into a ring with alternating bees and ladybugs as shown in diagram C. The final ring may be situated anywhere on the board within its outline. Remember that every continuous flight of a piece around another piece or pieces is counted as a single move. How many moves will you need to make a ring?

The Big Bee Challenge

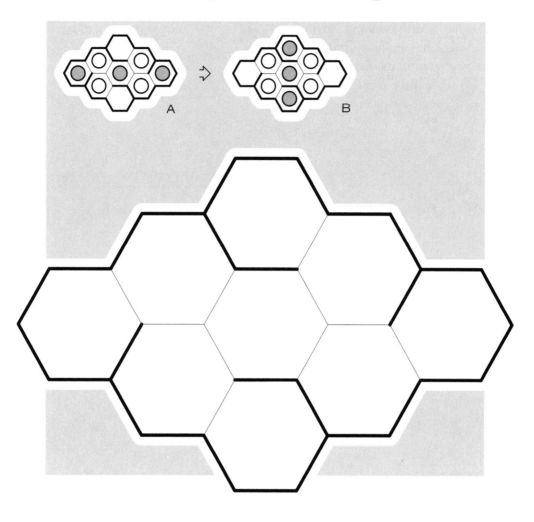

The above hexagonal board represents a small part of a beehive. In this beehive, place seven counters or coins as shown in diagram A. Now move your bees (counters) to the pattern shown in diagram B in nineteen single sliding moves.

Hexagonal Crisscross

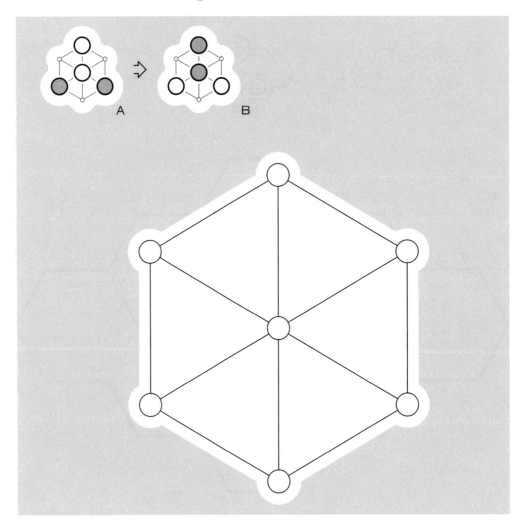

On the above grid, place four counters or coins as shown in diagram A. Performing one twin-move at a time, move the counters to the pattern shown in diagram B in six twin-moves.

The New Puzzle Classics

The Framed Move Challenge

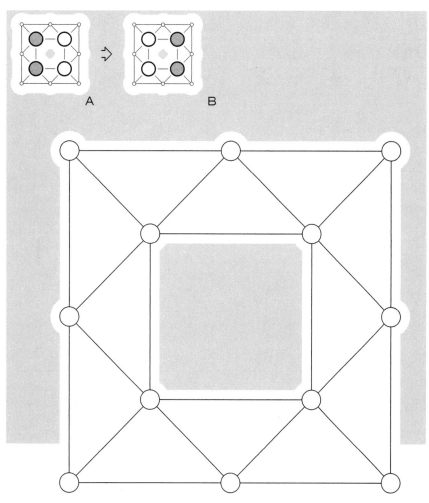

A   B

On the above grid, place four counters or coins as shown in diagram A. Performing one twin-move at a time, exchange counters as shown in diagram B. Can you do this in seven twin-moves?

Challenging Hopscotch

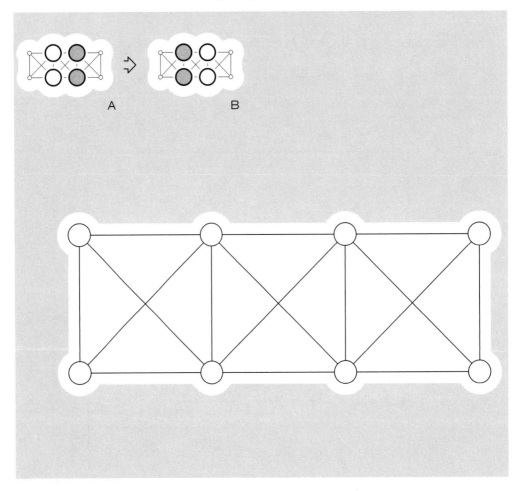

On the hopscotch grid, place four counters or coins as shown in diagram A. Performing one twin-move at a time, move counters to the pattern shown in diagram B in seven twin-moves.

The New Puzzle Classics

Two Joined Squares

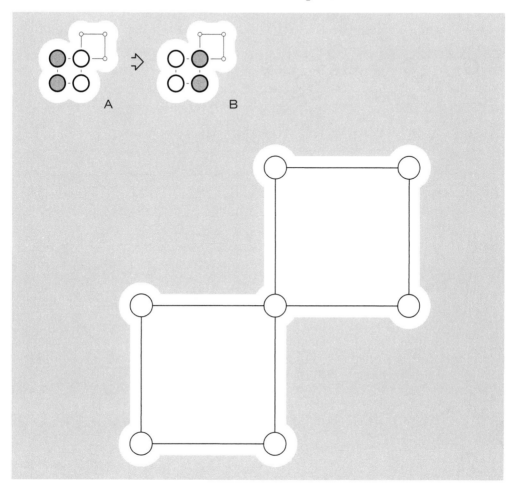

On the above grid, place four counters or coins as shown in diagram A. Performing one twin-move at a time, move counters to the pattern shown in diagram B in nine twin-moves.

Spinning Puzzle

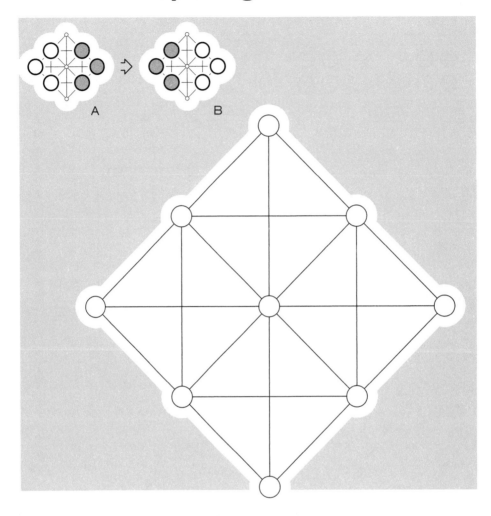

On the above grid, place six counters or coins as shown in diagram A. Performing one twin-move at a time, move counters to the pattern shown in diagram B in six twin-moves.

Eight Counters in Octagon

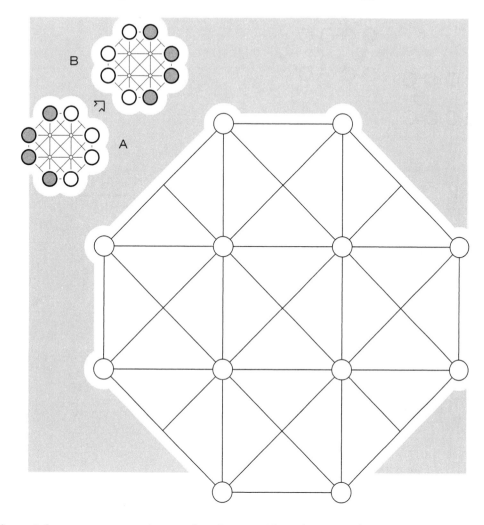

Place eight counters or coins on the above grid as shown in diagram A. Performing one twin-move at a time, move counters to the pattern shown in diagram B in eight twin-moves.

Hexa X-Changes

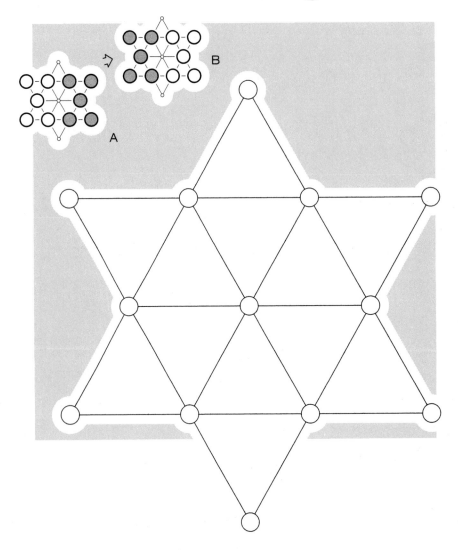

Place ten counters or coins on the star-like grid as shown in diagram A. Performing one twin-move at a time, move counters to the pattern shown in diagram B in ten twin-moves.

The New Puzzle Classics

Square Rearrangement

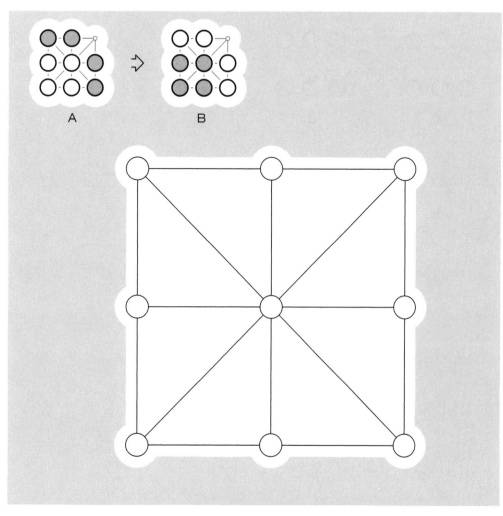

A   B

Place eight counters or coins on the above grid as shown in diagram A. Move counters to the pattern shown in diagram B in fifteen twin-moves.

Drumming Moves

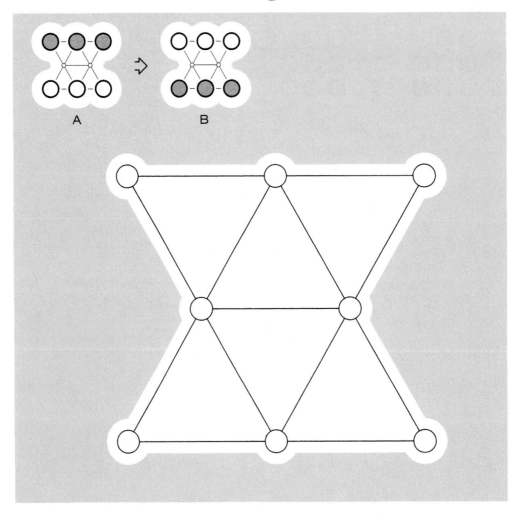

On the above grid, place six counters or coins as shown in diagram A. Performing one twin-move at a time, move counters to the pattern shown in diagram B in ten twin-moves.

The New Puzzle Classics

The Ancient Butterfly

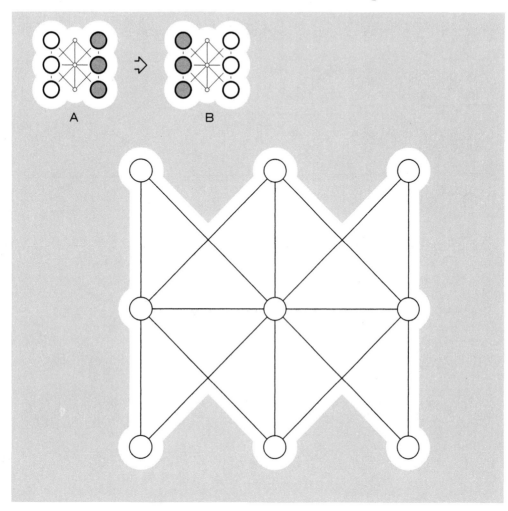

A

B

Place six counters or coins on the above grid as shown in diagram A. Performing one twin-move at a time, move counters to the pattern shown in diagram B in ten twin-moves.

Challenge of Cat Cradle

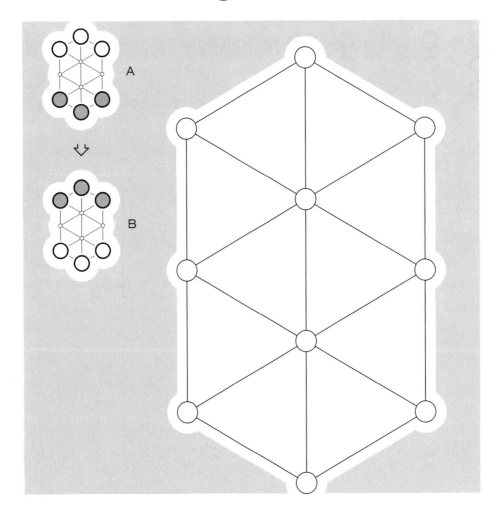

On the above grid, place six counters or coins as shown in diagram A. Your goal is to move counters to the pattern shown in diagram B in eight twin-moves, always performing one twin-move at a time.

The Fishbone Puzzle

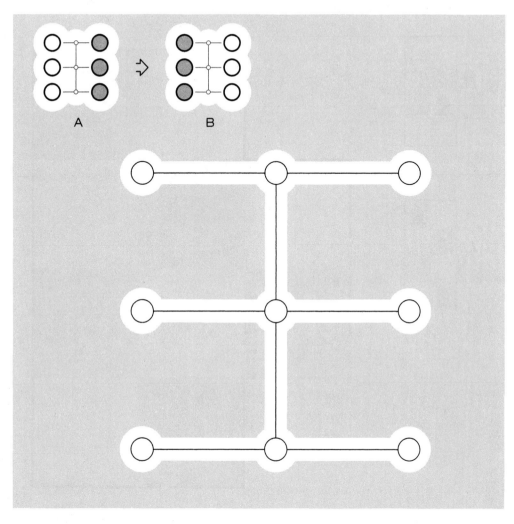

On the above grid, place six counters or coins as shown in diagram A. Performing one twin-move at a time, can you move counters to the pattern shown in diagram B in seventeen twin-moves?

The Knight Maze

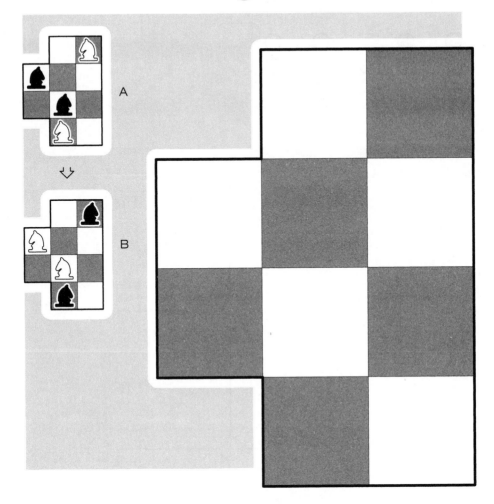

On the special chessboard shown above, place two pairs of knights (or two pairs of different coins)—two white and two black—as shown in diagram A. Performing only normal knight's moves, can you exchange the positions of white and black knights as shown in diagram B? Can you achieve this goal in less than twenty single leaps?

Knight's Maneuvers

A   B

Six chess knights (three white and three black) are placed on the special chessboard above as shown in diagram A. (Note that the chessboard lacks two central dark cells.) The object of this puzzle is to exchange the positions of the white and black knights as shown in diagram B by performing just normal knight's moves. Counting a consecutive series of leaps as one move, can you get to the final position in seven moves?

Knight-Rook Exchange

A

B

Two lines of chess pieces—three knights and three rooks—are positioned against each other as shown in diagram A. If you count a series of consecutive steps as one move, how many moves will you need to exchange the positions as shown in diagram B?

The New Puzzle Classics

All the King's Men

A   B

All six chess pieces—king, queen, rook, bishop, knight, and pawn—are gathered at the chess party as shown in diagram A. Now these chess pieces want to dance, observing all standard chess rules for their moves. How many moves are needed to get to the position shown in diagram B? One move may consist of a series of consecutive steps with the same piece. Remember that the pawn can move only forward, and never backward.

Cross the Lake

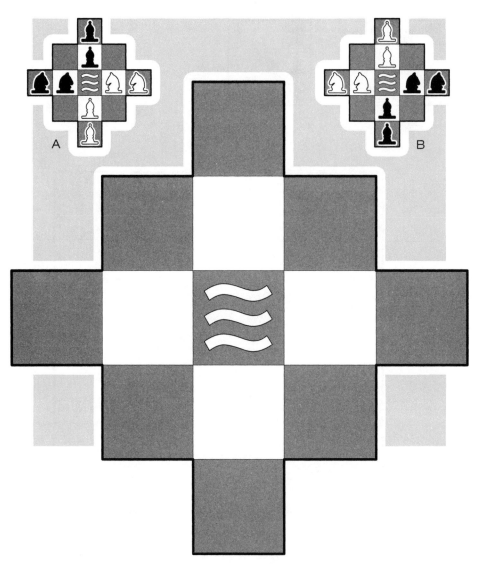

Eight chess pieces—four knights (two white and two black) and four bishops (two white and two black)—are placed on the special diagonal chessboard as shown in diagram A. The object is to exchange pairs of knights and bishops as shown in diagram B performing only normal knight's and bishop's moves. No piece may remain at the central cell ("lake"), but pieces may cross over it en route. Counting a consecutive series of steps as one move, can you perform this chess crossing in fourteen moves?

Change the Rooks

A   B

Eight chess pieces—two rooks, three knights, and three bishops—are placed on a 3 X 3 chessboard as shown in diagram A. The object is to exchange the rooks, and return the knights and bishops to their start position, as shown in diagram B. The black knights in the final position may be switched, if necessary, as well as the two black bishops. Can you solve this chess challenge in twenty moves?

Chapter **8**

CHALLENGING MIX

As the title of this chapter suggests, here you will find a mix of puzzles of varying degrees of difficulty. None of them, however, is meant to deliberately stumble or confuse. Again, logical reasoning, careful observation and analysis, and lateral thinking are the main tools that you will need to help you in the solving process. In any case, your patience will be rewarded with valuable and pleasant discoveries.

This chapter presents different puzzles that are devoted to unusual placements or moves of pieces in two and three dimensions; it is divided into two sections containing two-dimensional and three-dimensional puzzles, respectively. All the puzzles here use simple pieces similar to those in previous chapters: coins, matchsticks, simple wire pieces (such as staples), pieces of rope, shaped plates, different cubes, and common objects. A series of three-dimensional dissections are also included. Last, but not least, this chapter includes a series of newly devised puzzles with a matchstick snake.

The Matchstick Snake Puzzles

A matchstick snake is a continuous line of matchsticks, placed in a chain one after another, and connected at their ends. Every matchstick has its length equal to 1. (Every matchstick in this book is always considered as a mathematical object—a line with length 1.) Every matchstick must have its direction given from the previous one and turned around their common point at multiples of 30 or 45 degrees. These matchstick snakes are called "degree-30 snakes" and "degree-45 snakes," respectively. Thus, all angles between the adjacent matchsticks for a degree-30 snake must be 30, 60, 90, 120, 150, or 180 degrees only, and for a degree-45 snake—45, 90, 135, or 180 degrees.

The object of all matchstick snake puzzles is to form the longest possible snake within the boundaries (including its border) of some two- or three-dimensional shape. The length of any matchstick snake is counted as the total number of matchsticks that make the snake. A matchstick snake consisting of N matchsticks is described as a Snake-N. Matchsticks must not cross each other, and a final snake—its math line—must not touch itself at any point. Snakes should not be closed in a loop. For some puzzles a background grid (or special line pattern) is provided for your convenience; matchsticks should go along the lines of the grid, or be parallel to some of its lines.

The matchstick snake puzzle has been widely discussed within the international puzzle community, and on the Web you can find an astonishing number of new and exciting discoveries that derive from such a seemingly simple puzzle type. In particular, large collections of discoveries and solutions to the matchstick snake puzzle are presented at Ed Pegg Jr.'s MathPuzzle.Com Web site (www.mathpuzzle.com), and Erich Friedman's Math Magic Web site (www.stetson.edu/~efriedma/mathmagic). In this chapter, the most interesting matchstick snake puzzles are presented. Please note that these puzzles can be very addictive.

The Five Y's

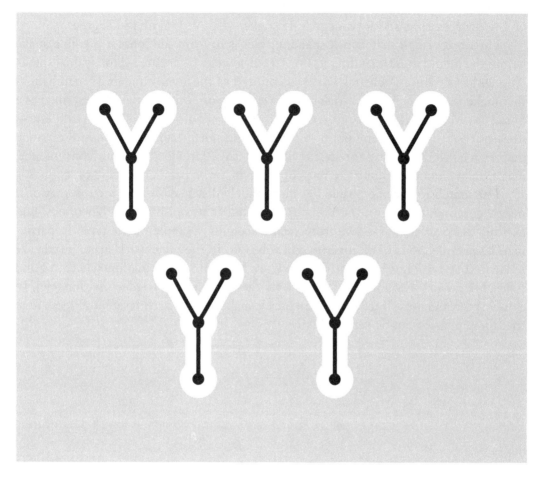

The arms of each of the five Y's above have the same length (1 unit), and the angles between them are, starting at the top and moving clockwise, 60, 150, and 150 degrees. Place the five Y's on a flat surface to form four equilateral triangles of the same size. You may form additional shapes within your composition, but no free (loose) ends of Y's may remain. Y's must join one another at their nodes only, and several nodes may meet at a point. Y's may not cross each other. As a warm-up, try to solve the same puzzle using just four Y's.

Six Wire Corners

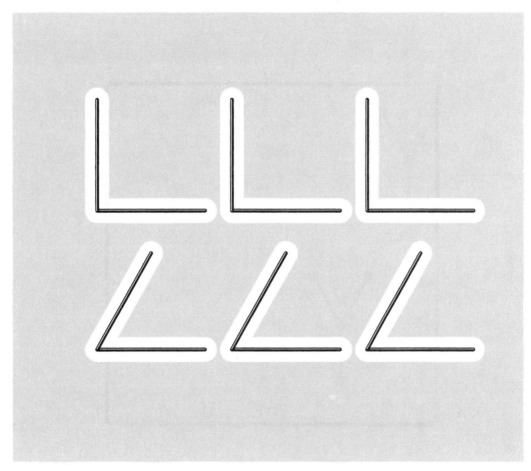

Six pieces of wire (2 units of length each) were bent into six L-corners as shown in the illustration. Three of them form angles of 90 degrees between their arms; the other three form angles of 60 degrees.

Puzzle 1. Use all six corners to form three equilateral triangles of the same size, and two squares of the same size. All of the triangles and squares must have sides of 1 unit of length.

Puzzle 2. Use the six corners to form three squares of the same size (with sides of 1 unit of length). You may form triangles or other shapes in addition to the three squares.

Note that no loose ends may remain in your solutions in these puzzles.

The Eight Stick Challenge

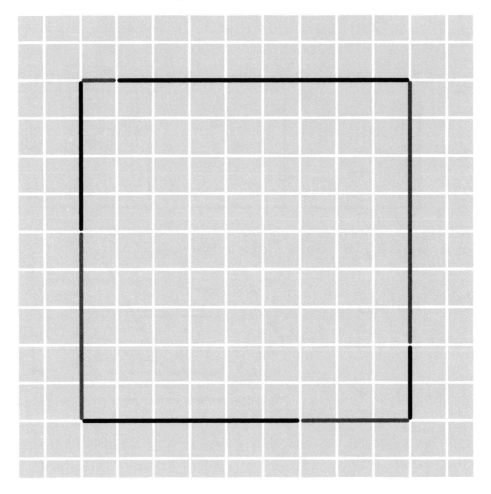

Eight different sticks, of lengths of 1 through 8 units, can be laid along the lines of a square grid to fence a 9 X 9 square with the *maximum* area of 81 square units as shown in the above diagram. How can these eight sticks fence the *minimal* area that will be exactly *inscribed* into a 9 X 9 square? Sticks may neither cross nor overlap, even partially. A new fence should run along the lines of the grid, be continuous and closed, and use all eight sticks without any loose ends. *Hint:* Its area consists of less than 22 square units.

The New Puzzle Classics

The Fence Puzzle

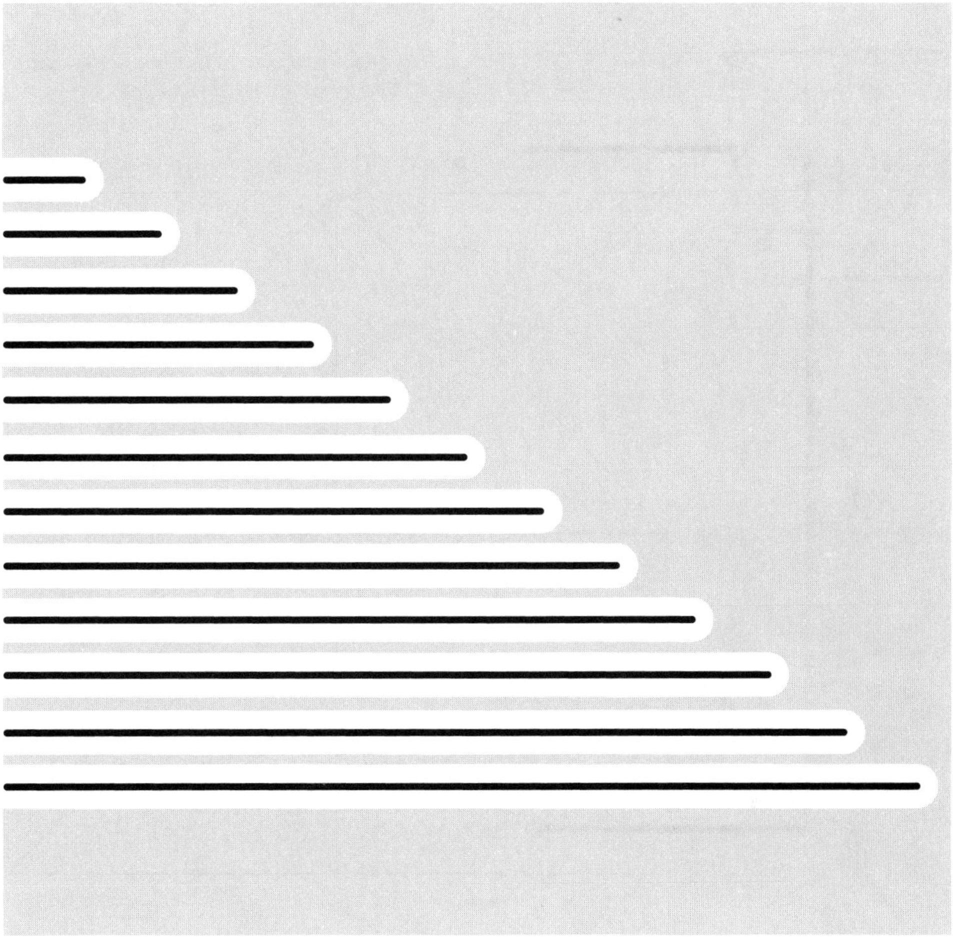

Using twelve sticks of different lengths—from 1 to 12 units—form a polygon with the *largest* possible area. Angles between each pair of sticks must be 45, 90, 135, or 180 degrees. All the sticks at their full length must be used. After you solve this puzzle, try to form a polygon with the *smallest* area using the same twelve sticks and allowed angles shown above.

Nick Baxter has proposed an elegant version of the puzzle without using 180-degree angles. Can you solve both of the above challenges observing Nick's rule?

The Neo Matchstick Snake

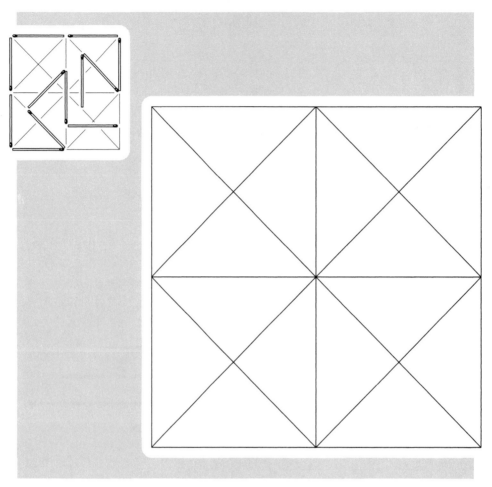

The object of this challenge is to form the longest possible degree-45 matchstick snake exactly within a 2 X 2 square (including its border). It is easy to find a Snake-12 (as shown in the above example), Snake-13, or Snake-14, but there is an even longer one—Snake-15. Can you find it? Another (and much harder!) challenge within a 2 X 2 square is to find the longest possible degree-30 matchstick snake. Oyvind Tafjord discovered, using his computer program, that there are sixty-four degree-30 Snake-19s, and two unbelievable degree-30 Snake-20s. Susan Hoover found one of the latter by hand! Can you discover one of them?

Polygons for the Matchstick Snake

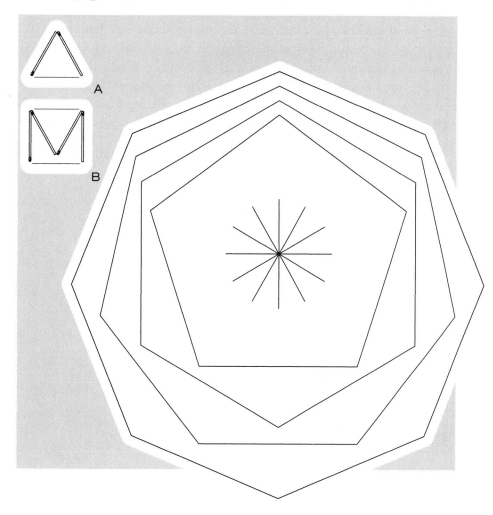

It is easy to build the longest degree-30 matchstick snakes within the simplest regular polygons—an equilateral triangle and square. They are shown in diagrams A and B, respectively. For a square, there are several different solutions; can you find them?

Continuing to play with a degree-30 snake within further regular polygons, it is possible to find a Snake-6 within a pentagon, a Snake-11 within a hexagon, a Snake-14 within a heptagon, and a Snake-18 within an octagon. Can you find all of them?

Can you beat any of these results? Keep in mind that while building snakes, you may use the outlines of the polygons as well.

A special combined diagram that includes four polygons simultaneously is provided to solve the puzzle using standard matchsticks directly on the page. Simply choose a polygon, outline it with a pencil, and then build a matchstick snake within it, disregarding the lines of the other polygons. The line star in the middle of the diagram is depicted to show all possible directions for placing matchsticks. To solve the puzzles, you may copy any of the polygons on a separate sheet of paper.

The Matchstick Snake in a Circle

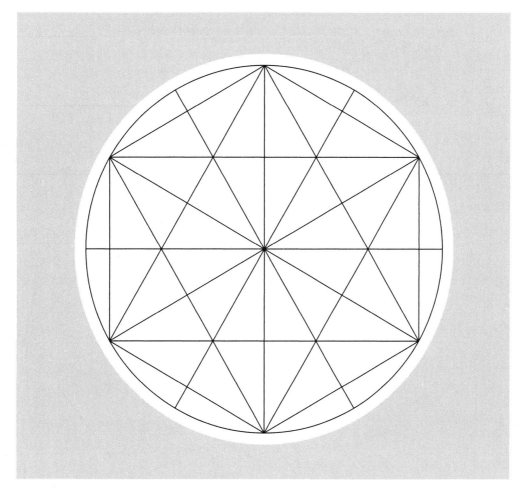

The longest matchstick snake within a regular hexagon is a degree-30 Snake-11. As you can see, the circle with a unit radius shown above includes such a hexagon, but now it provides an additional place for one more matchstick. The challenge is to discover a degree-30 Snake-12 within the circle. Can you do this?

Place & Turn

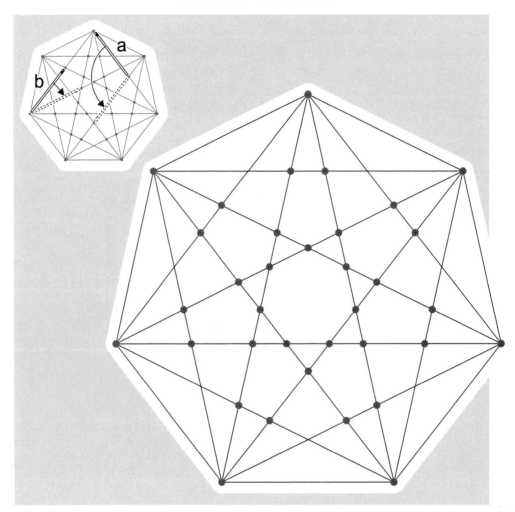

The grid shown above is based on a regular heptagon with all of its vertices connected with one other in all possible combinations. Thirty-five nodes of the grid (marked with dots) are used for the purposes of this puzzle. The object is to place as many matchsticks as you can fit onto the grid. Every matchstick has its length equal to a side of the heptagon.

You should place every matchstick onto the grid as described herein. *First*, a matchstick must be placed on a free line of the grid between exactly two nodes; the distance between them must equal to a side of the heptagon. At the same time, the matchstick may lie over other nodes. *Second*, you *must* turn the matchstick around any of its ends, and finish on a *free neighboring* line as shown in the upper left diagram—matchsticks **a** and **b**. Thus, both start and finish lines on the grid must have a common node: a point for turning. After the turn, a matchstick must finish exactly between two nodes, with a distance of a side of the heptagon between them. No other matchstick(s) should lie in the way of the turning matchstick. For example, in the upper left diagram you may not turn matchstick **a** into its finish position if matchstick **b** was placed on the grid and turned to a new position first. It is possible, though, to place and turn these matchsticks in the opposite order—first **a**, then **b**. You must turn matchsticks within the grid only; you may not use the space outside it. How many matchsticks can you place on the grid based on the above conditions?

Two Weaving Loops

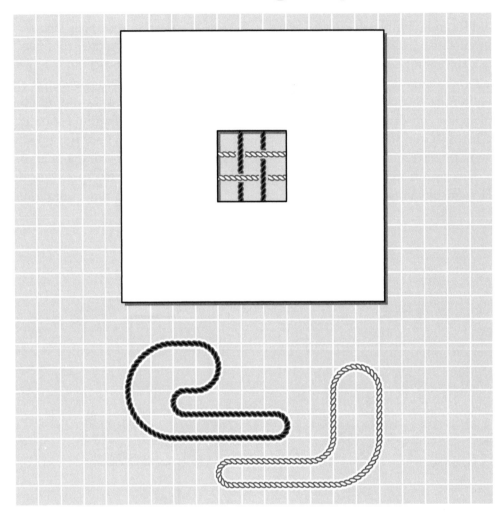

There are two rope loops shown in the illustration above. These loops were inter-woven (without breaking them), and after that the whole composition was covered with a square sheet of paper with a square window in it so that within the window you can see fragments of the ropes as shown in the upper illustration. The challenge is to reveal the whole pattern of the rope composition, bearing in mind that none of the loops crosses itself, each loop crosses and interweaves with the other loop only, and they cross each other less than ten times.

The New Puzzle Classics

The Fenced Knight's Tour

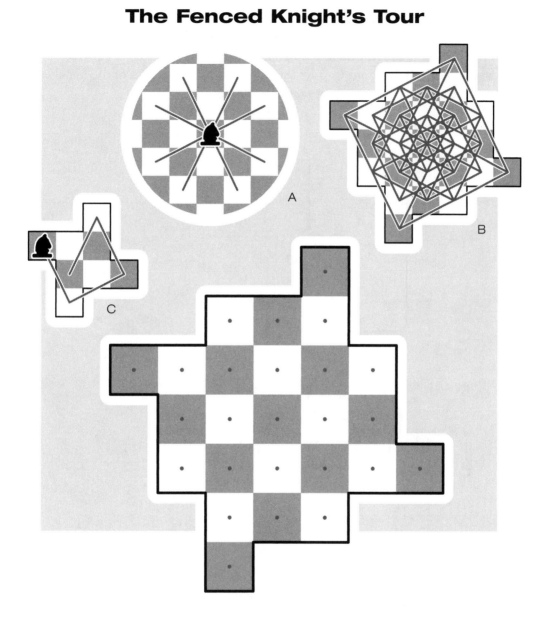

A

B

C

Diagram A shows all possible moves of a chess knight from a cell, considering every leap of the knight as a straight line segment. Diagram B shows the full graph of knight's moves on the special chessboard shown in the middle. Thus, any tour of a knight on this board always will be enclosed within a square boundary formed with the outer segments of such a tour.

The challenge is to find the longest noncrossing tour a knight can perform on this board within the square boundary (including its border) shown in diagram B. A small example of the longest noncrossing knight's tour within a 1 X 1 square boundary is shown in diagram C. The small black dots in the cells of the big chessboard are provided to help you plot your knight's tour.

The Red Triangle Puzzle

Take three cubes and for each of them draw one bold line (say, in red) along the diagonal on any of its faces, to get three identical cubes as shown above. Using these three cubes, form an equilateral triangle from the three bold lines drawn on the cubes. The final construction, when built on the table, must be self-supported; that is, it must be stable without support of any kind. How can the red triangle be formed?

The Yellow Cube Puzzle

This puzzle consists of six identical cubes with one yellow (shaded) face each, as shown above. The object of this challenge is to place all the cubes onto a flat surface (say, a table) so that they form a yellow cube; all of its faces must be yellow. The final construction, when finished, must be self-supported; that is, it must be stable without your help or support of any kind. Can you discover how to form the yellow cube?

The Softy Challenge

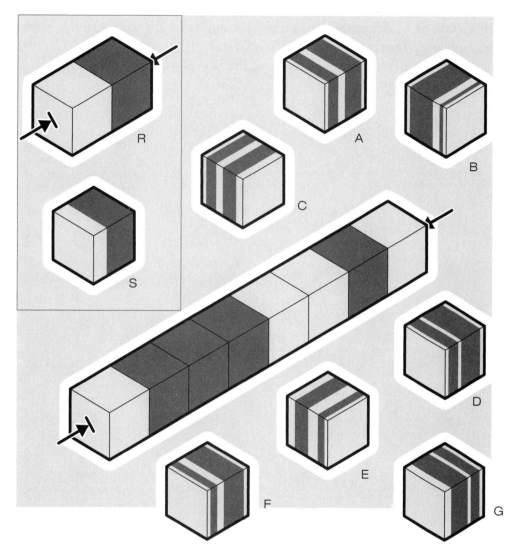

There are two types of 1 X 1 X 1 foam cubes—one type is more soft (shown as light), while the other is more tough (shown as dark). Tough cubes are half as compressible as soft cubes. If two cubes of different types form a short 1 X 1 X 2 block as shown in left illustration R, and they are squeezed into a 1 X 1 X 1 cube, you will get the cube shown in the illustration S. This combined, two-colored cube consists of two parts—light (soft) and dark (tough)—with their thicknesses measured by a 1:2 ratio.

If we take eight different cubes, build up a long 1 X 1 X 8 block like that shown in the middle, and compress it into a 1 X 1 X 1 cube again, which of the seven two-colored cubes (A–G) will we get? Note that the new two-colored cube might be rotated after squeezing.

The Wooden Patterns Puzzle

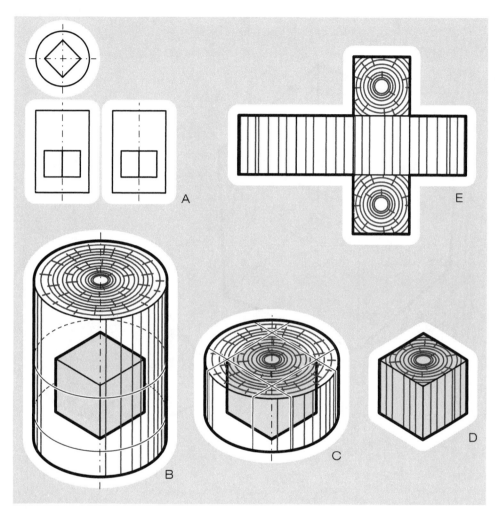

Imagine that you want to cut out a cube from a circular log. Diagram A and illustrations B through D show a possible way to do this. As you can see, two opposite faces of the cube are perpendicular to the long axis of the log, and the cube's center coincides with this axis. On the cube, you will recognize two different types of patterns—a "circular" pattern on the faces that are perpendicular to the log's axis, and a "linear" pattern on the remaining four faces, which are parallel to this axis. (See illustration D and right diagram E, representing a layout of the cube.) The challenge is to discover how a cube should be oriented within a log in order to get a cube with identical patterns on all six of its faces.

The Cone Challenge

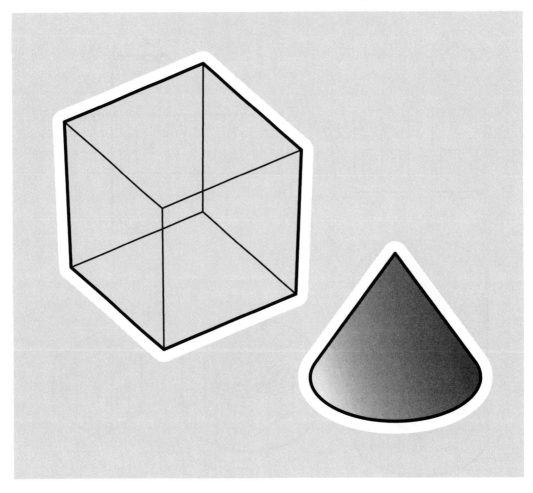

A circular cone is placed fully inside a 1 X 1 X 1 cube. What is the largest possible diameter of its circular base? What is its maximal height? How many copies of such a cone may be placed inside the cube?

The Plate Packing (4K-5I)

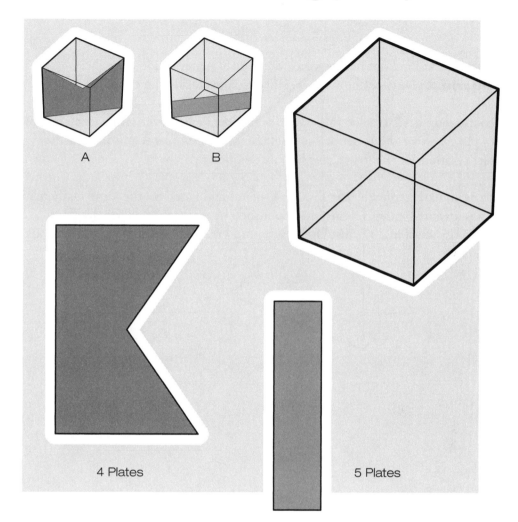

A

B

4 Plates

5 Plates

This is a two-in-one puzzle. The object is to put a set of thin plates inside a 1 X 1 X 1 cube. The first set (K-set) consists of four K-shaped plates as seen in the above left diagram. The K-plate has its short side length 1, and its long side is equal to the diagonal of the cube face. How it fits inside the cube is shown in the illustration A. The second set (I-set) includes five narrow rectangular I-shaped plates. The I-plate has its short side measuring one-third of the cube edge, and its long side is equal to the diagonal of the cube face. Illustration B shows how the I-plate fits inside the cube.

Puzzle 1: Find out how to place the four K-plates inside the cube.
Puzzle 2: Discover how to place five I-plates inside the cube.

Of course, you have to solve these puzzles independently, every time using just one set of plates, either the K-set or the I-set. *Hint:* Illustrations A and B show the correct position for the first plates in both solutions.

A puzzle similar to **puzzle 1** with four K-plates and based on the same mathematical idea was invented independently and published by a Japanese puzzle designer Hirokazu Iwasawa in 2004 just after I submitted the final manuscript of this book to the publisher.

The Paper Cube Puzzle

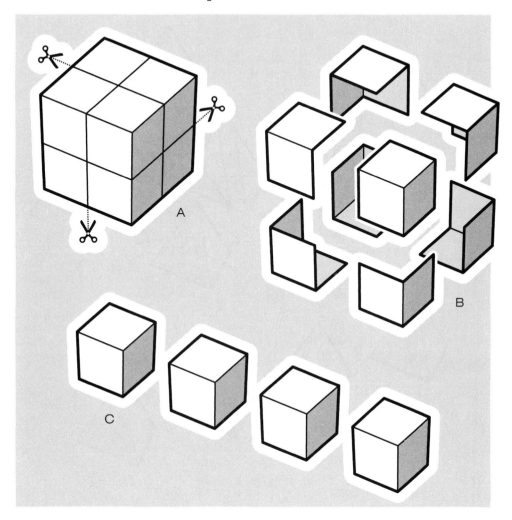

It is possible to cut a paper cube (empty inside) as shown in illustration A into eight equal pieces shown in illustration B. Now you can easily pair them up into four *equal* smaller cubes (illustration C). The challenge is to find out how to divide a paper cube into twenty pieces of only three types, which can form three *different* cubes; every cube will consist of its own type of equal pieces. New pieces may be neither bent nor folded/unfolded; they must be used in the new cubes exactly as formed after your cuts. Pieces may rotate, but may not overlap.

The Paper Tetrahedron Puzzle

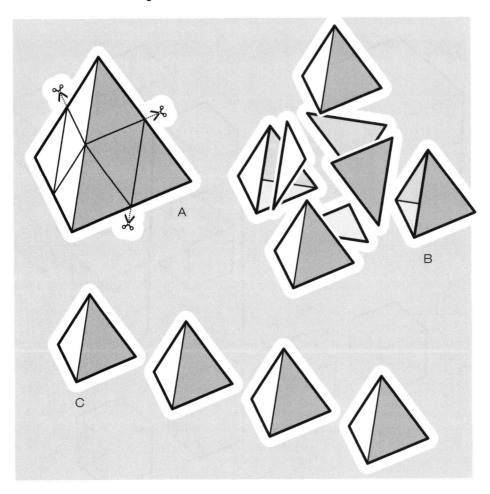

If you cut a regular paper tetrahedron (empty inside) along the lines as shown in illustration A, you will get eight pieces—four equal caps and four equal equilateral triangles—shown in illustration B. They may be paired up into the *four* equal small tetrahedrons shown in illustration C. The challenge is to divide a regular paper tetrahedron into eight pieces that can form *three* new regular tetrahedrons. Some of these new tetrahedrons may be of the same size. New pieces may be neither bent nor folded/unfolded; they must be used exactly as formed after your cuts. Pieces may rotate, but may not overlap.

The New Puzzle Classics

Two Similar Tubes

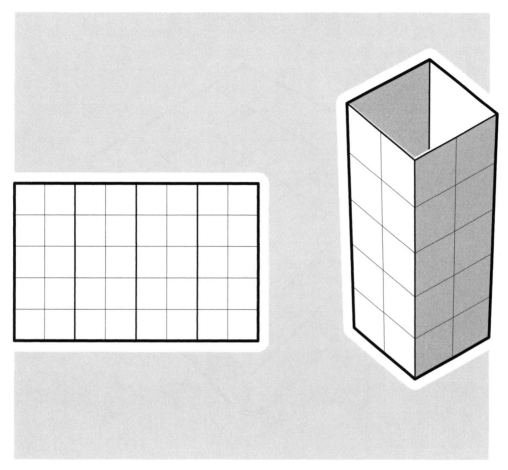

A paper tube of dimensions 2 X 2 X 5 is shown in the right illustration. Its layout is shown on the left; you may use it while solving the puzzle. The object of this challenge is to divide the tube into four parts—cutting along the lines—so that they may then be rearranged into two new tubes similar to each other, although not necessarily of the same size. This means that these two new tubes must be proportionate to each other in size. The thickness of the tubes' walls and the pattern on them do not matter. The tube (and its parts) may neither be bent nor folded/unfolded; the parts of the tube must be used in new tubes exactly as they were formed after your cuts. Parts may rotate, but may not overlap.

The Challenging Block

You are an architect, and your task is to create a universal project for a single town block. You are to build up a 4 X 4 square area with buildings that cover any area within your block, from one single square of dimensions 1 X 1 up to 16 squares. You start with 16 single cubic 1 X 1 X 1 buildings, which can cover exactly 16 squares of your area as shown in the bird's-eye view above.

   The challenge is to divide all 16 single cubic buildings into three groups, and then join them together into three *different* rectangular buildings which allow you to finish your project. In other words, you should have three parallelepipeds with which you can cover (using one, two, or all three of them) any area in the range of one through 16 single squares within the 4 X 4 block. You may turn the buildings as you wish by placing them on any of their faces, but you may not stack them up.

Invert a Color Brick

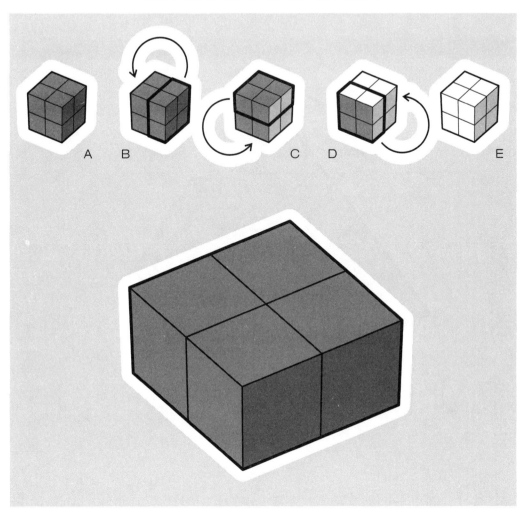

If you cut a fully colored cube into eight smaller cubes, and then rearrange them as shown in illustrations A through E, you will form a new cube so that all colored parts are inside. You now have a flat square solid brick (half of a cube) with its surface fully colored in one color. Divide the brick into six simple pieces so that you can rearrange them into another rectangular brick with its surface fully uncolored. In other words, all the colored parts must be fully hidden inside this new brick.

Hide the Color

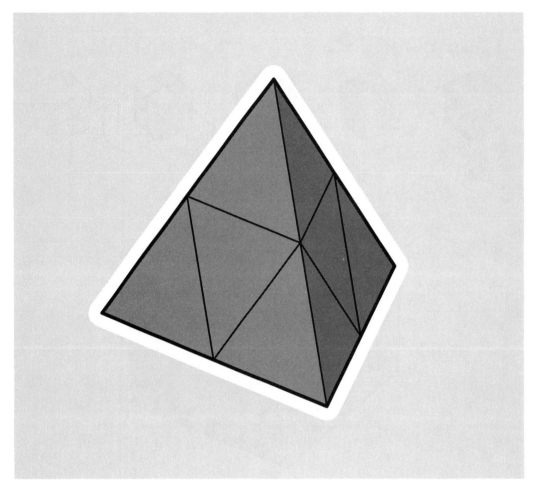

This color-inverting puzzle is a variant of the previous one with a colored brick, but with a fully colored regular solid tetrahedron. First, divide the tetrahedron into two pieces identical in color and size. Then take one of these two pieces and again divide it into two smaller ones of the exact same size. You will now have three pieces. Rearrange them to form a solid shape with its surface fully uncolored. In other words, all colored parts of the tetrahedron must be fully hidden inside this new solid.

The New Puzzle Classics

Cubical Inversion

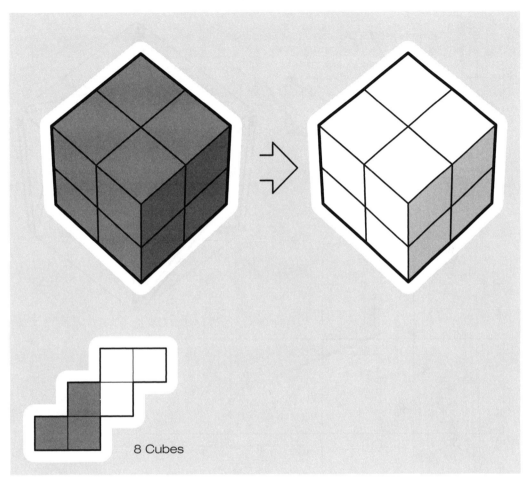

8 Cubes

The fully dark 2 X 2 X 2 cube shown above at left consists of eight small 1 X 1 X 1 cubes that have three dark and three light faces each. The layout of such a small cube is shown just beneath the 2 X 2 X 2 dark cube. The challenge is to invert the dark cube into the fully light cube (as shown on the right) by moving the small cubes in pairs of two adjacent cubes at each move. You may choose any pair that you can take (grasp) with your thumb and index finger, and move it orthogonally (without turning or rotating) to its new position, where this pair will touch at least two of the other cubes. Cubes may touch each other only with their whole sides. Can you invert the dark cube in a sequence of six pair-moves?

The Matchstick Snake on a Cube

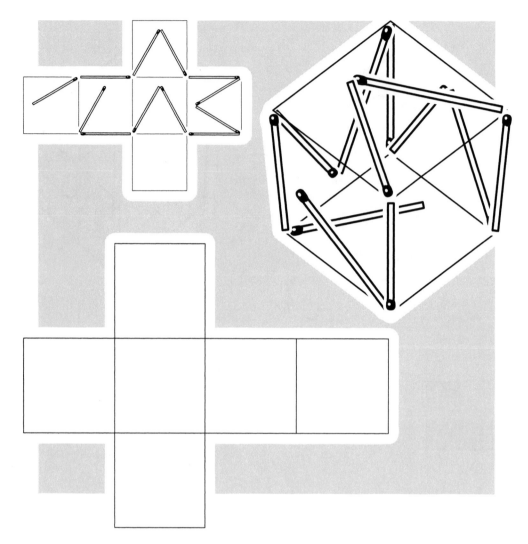

The above illustrations show a degree-30 Snake-12 on the surface of a 1 X 1 X 1 unit cube; the uppermost left illustration shows the snake on the cube's layout. There is a degree-30 Snake-15 on the surface of a unit cube. Can you find it? The empty layout is provided to mark matchsticks while you solve the puzzle. Note that since this matchstick snake is a degree-30 snake, *all* the angles between adjacent matchsticks must be 30, 60, 90, 120, 150, and 180 degrees only, including those places where the snake crawls over the cube's edges from one of its faces to another.

SOLUTIONS

This part of the book includes detailed solutions to all the puzzles from Chapters 1 through 8, and is as important a part of the book as the chapters themselves. Even peeping at the desired solution (after a solver has spent some time trying to solve a particular challenge, and is ready to give up) provides an educational effect satisfying the solver's interest to get to the core of the puzzle idea, and may foster a sense of satisfaction and accomplishment.

Solutions to the puzzles were found by the author, unless otherwise stated. (SGJ means Serhiy Grabarchuk Jr.) Some of the puzzles may have alternative solutions not shown in the book.

Puzzling Dissections

Solutions to the dissection puzzles are shown in the same manner as the puzzles. Dividing lines at every cut shape and different shadings for single parts are added. In some cases a particular shape's pattern was not shown in order to clarify the solution to that challenge.

Dot-Connections

Solutions to these puzzles are shown in different ways. For some puzzles, lines connecting some set of objects are drawn directly over these objects or, in some cases, around them. For other puzzles, if there is a given set of some route's parts, they are simply placed together so that the final dot-connecting routes appear. Additionally, some puzzles have some shadings or differently colored parts that clarify their solutions.

Matchsticks & Coins

In the solutions to matchstick puzzles, matchsticks that have not been moved from their original positions are shown in their original form. Black matchsticks show the places where the matchsticks have been moved to. Dotted matchsticks show the places where the matchsticks have been moved/removed from. To make some solutions clearer, dotted lines and/or grids and shadings are added.

For coin puzzles, every solution is presented as a sequence of diagrams that show consecutive positions of coins with every subsequent move highlighted. The final position is always marked with "F." A coin (or a group of coins) that is moving is always outlined with a bold line. Its destination place is always shown with a dotted outline. For puzzles with changing of coin placement, their solutions are shown as the final placements, with necessary additional arrows or lines marked. In these cases, dotted coins show the places where the coins have been moved from. Coins outlined with bold lines show the new places where they have been moved to.

Witty Patterns

Solutions to these puzzles are presented in different ways appropriate to the particular types of challenges. Some solutions simply straightforwardly present the final positions of given sets of pieces arranged together on their respective boards or into some composition according to given rules. Many solutions utilize shadings or differently colored parts to highlight their ideas and to clarify the solutions. Where necessary, solutions are provided with detailed comments and additional diagrams.

Words & Numbers

Solutions to dissection, matchstick, and pattern puzzles in this chapter are shown in ways described above for their respective types of puzzles. Other challenges are provided with detailed explanations and diagrams.

Origami Puzzles

In the solutions to the origami puzzles, the following symbols and marks are used to show folds and other manipulations with paper sheets:

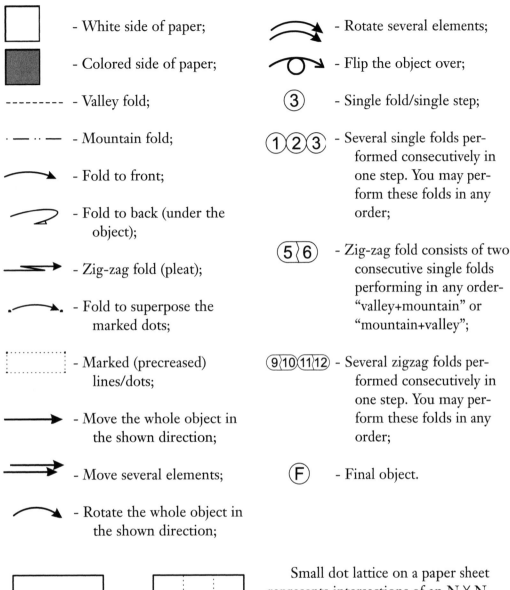

- White side of paper;

- Colored side of paper;

--------- - Valley fold;

·—··— - Mountain fold;

- Fold to front;

- Fold to back (under the object);

- Zig-zag fold (pleat);

- Fold to superpose the marked dots;

- Marked (precreased) lines/dots;

- Move the whole object in the shown direction;

- Move several elements;

- Rotate the whole object in the shown direction;

- Rotate several elements;

- Flip the object over;

③ - Single fold/single step;

①②③ - Several single folds performed consecutively in one step. You may perform these folds in any order;

⑤⑥ - Zig-zag fold consists of two consecutive single folds performing in any order- "valley+mountain" or "mountain+valley";

⑨⑩⑪⑫ - Several zigzag folds performed consecutively in one step. You may perform these folds in any order;

Ⓕ - Final object.

Small dot lattice on a paper sheet represents intersections of an $N \times N$ grid which is used as a basic pattern to start and perform all folds in every particular origami puzzle. Every $N \times N$ grid can be precreased or marked out on a paper sheet before you start to fold it.

Solutions   **243**

Tricky Moves

Every solution to challenges with moving pieces (either counters or coins) is presented as a sequence of diagrams that show consecutive positions of moving pieces, given move-by-move. The final position is always marked with "F." A piece (or a group of pieces) that is moving is always outlined with a bold line. Its destination place is always shown with a dotted outline. In puzzles with twin-moves, sometimes one of the destination places is also a starting place for another piece from the moving pair, so in these cases you will see just one dotted outline. Another destination place can be easily spotted just next to it.

Solutions to chess puzzles contain start and finish diagrams shown at left and right, respectively, with a move sequence placed between them. Every move consists of several letters (referring to the letters in the cells of the diagrams), which mean starting, intermediate, and finishing cells. Also, there are letters that indicate which chess piece is moving; the "K" means king, "Q": queen, "R": rook, "B": bishop, "Kn": knight, and "P": pawn.

Challenging Mix

Since puzzles in this chapter differ widely, solutions to them are presented in a number of ways, including some described for the previous chapters. Mostly, the solutions contain detailed explanations and diagrams. For most solutions to puzzles with matchstick snakes, only their graphs are shown.

Puzzling Dissections—Solutions

THE NAUTILUS PUZZLE

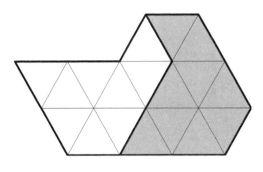

THE CHALLENGE OF THE PYRAMID

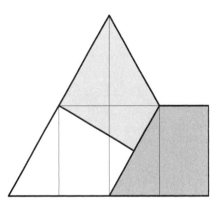

TRIPLE CUT

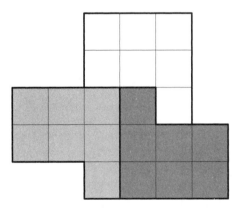

CRACKER DISSECTION

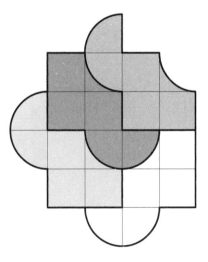

DIVIDE THE GRID

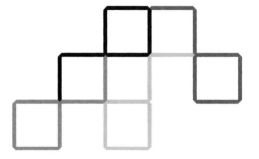

THE Q-GRID PUZZLE

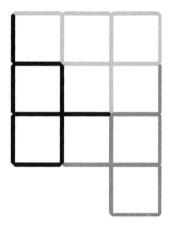

THE SHARK CHALLENGE

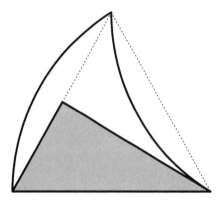

MANTA'S PUZZLE

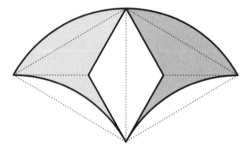

THE TRIANGLE TABLE PUZZLE

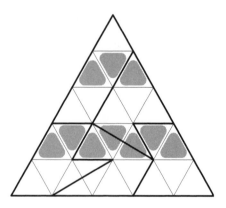

The New Puzzle Classics

CHALLENGING DIAMOND

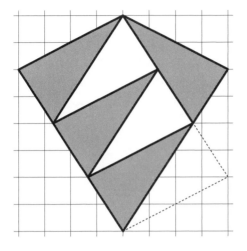

STAR & CROSS

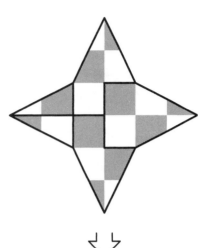

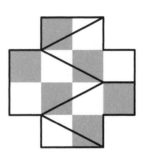

THE CHECKERED Q

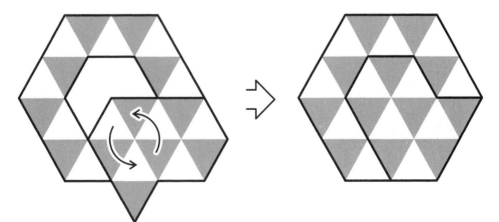

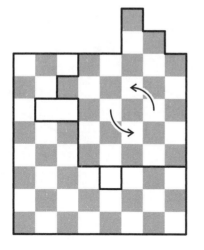 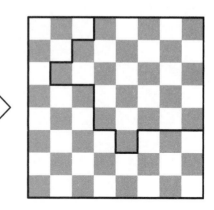

CHECKERED MULTIPLICATION

To turn a 4 X 4 checkerboard into a "standard" 8 X 8 one, you should cut it into 25 simple pieces (of four different kinds) as shown below left. Then, you have many ways to assemble them into an 8 X 8 checkerboard; one of them is shown in the illustration below right.

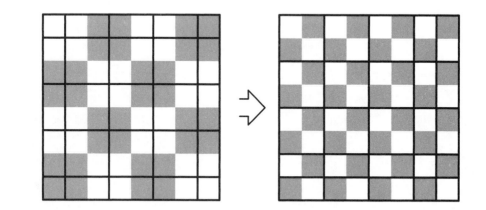

THE SHIELD CHALLENGE

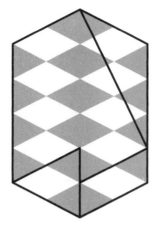

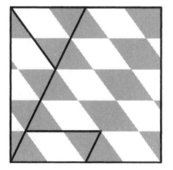

TRIANGLE ADDITION

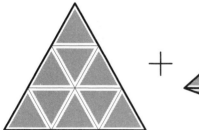 +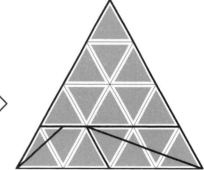

RESTORE THE BUTTON

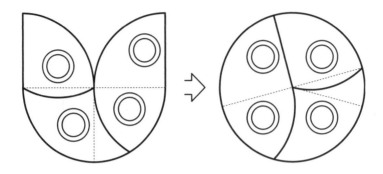

MOLECULAR DISSECTION

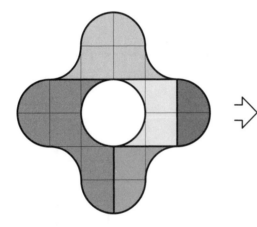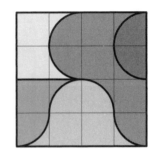

DRAGON SQUARING

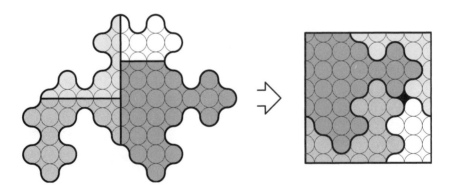

THE PECTORAL PUZZLE

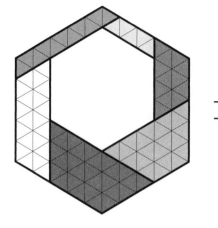
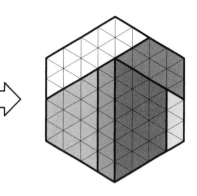

SQUARING THE ARROW

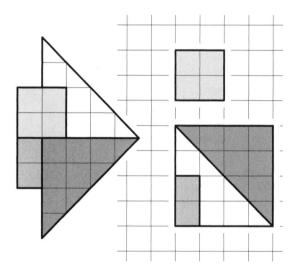

CHRISTMAS TREE & SQUARE

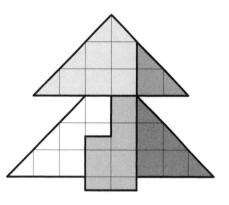

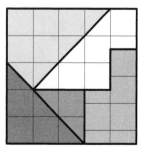

GRID CHANGES

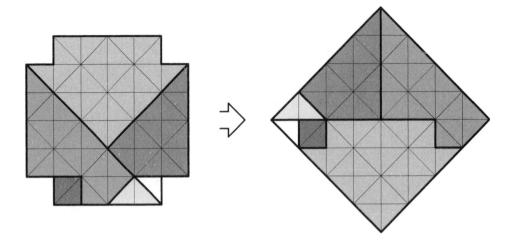

SQUARED EIGHT

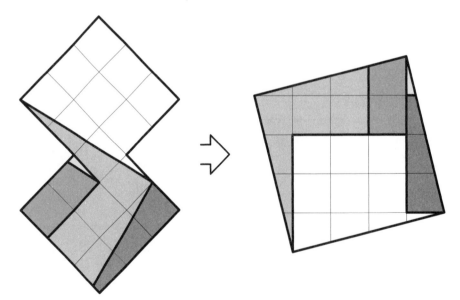

Dot-Connections—Solutions

THE FLOWER ARROW

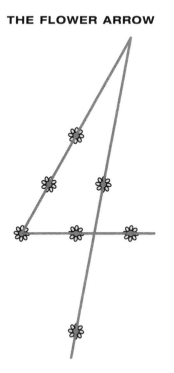

JOIN EIGHT MARBLES

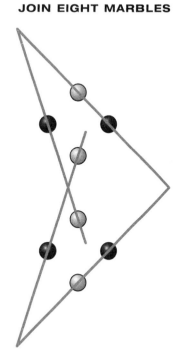

STARS & SPIRALS

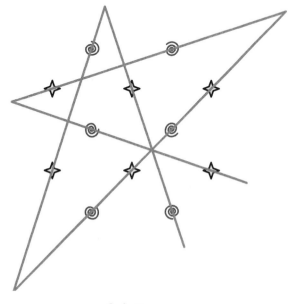

THE PUZZLE CONSTELLATION

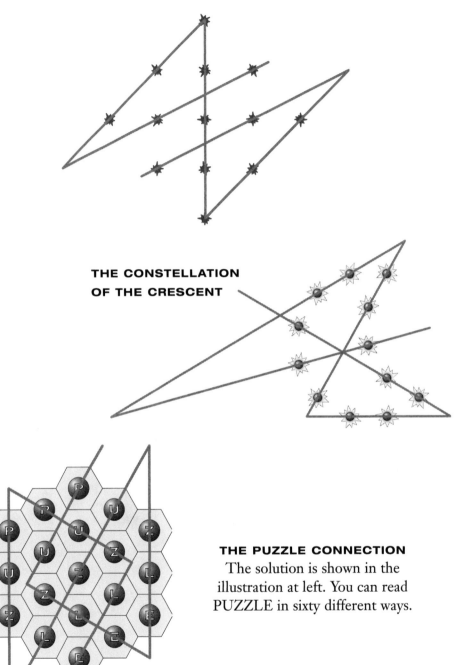

THE CONSTELLATION
OF THE CRESCENT

THE PUZZLE CONNECTION
The solution is shown in the illustration at left. You can read PUZZLE in sixty different ways.

The New Puzzle Classics

IN THE DOMINO MOOD

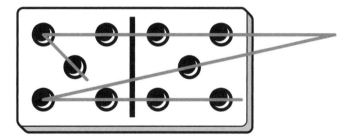

Solution 1—Open Route

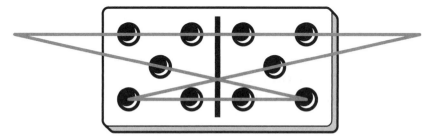

Solution 2—Closed Route

DICEY CONNECTIONS

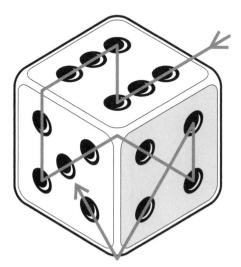

BOUQUET OF BULBS

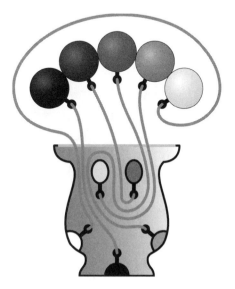

BUTTONS, NEEDLES & THREADS

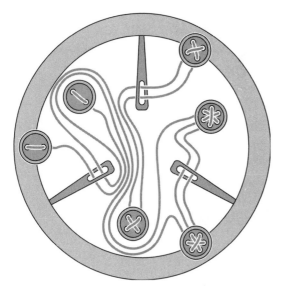

THE MATCH CONNECTIONS

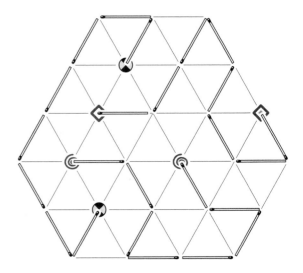

ARROWHEAD CONNECTION

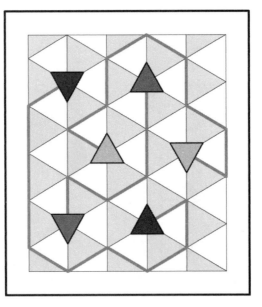

KNIGHT'S TETRA-CONNEXIONS

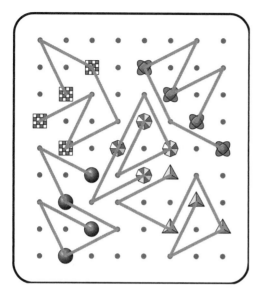

THE BILLIARD BALL TRAP CHALLENGE

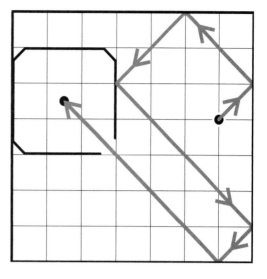

THE UNICURSAL TANGRAM BIRD

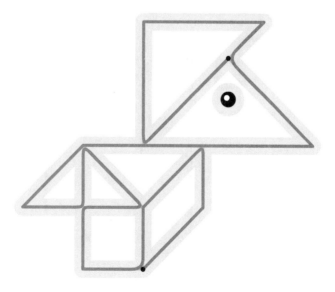

THE DOUBLE UNICURSAL GRID

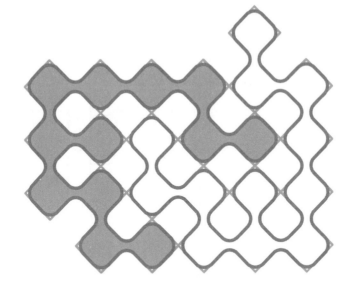

THE DRAGON CIRCUIT

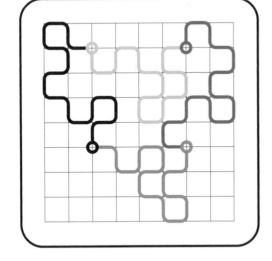

THE SEVEN DEPOTS PUZZLE

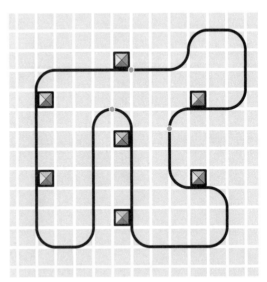

THE TWISTING PAPER SNAKE

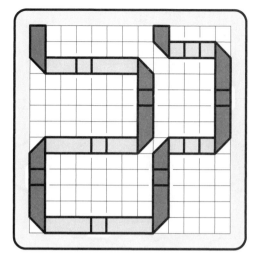

THE RACETRACK PUZZLE

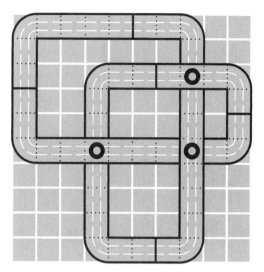

THE COLOR CANDY CHAIN

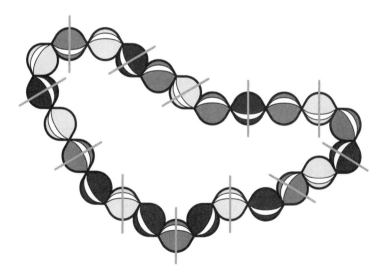

THE CHALLENGE OF THE GREEN LINE

THE COLOR COMB ZIGZAG

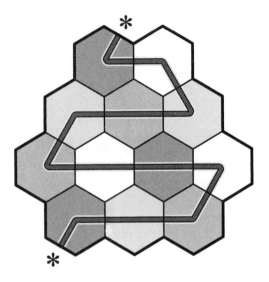

LINES-THROUGH-DOTS

b	c	*c*	b	d
e	*c*	d	*a*	e
a	e	*e*	b	*e*
a	*d*	c	*d*	c
b	d	*a*	b	a

The New Puzzle Classics

Matchsticks & Coins—Solutions

CAT & CHAIR

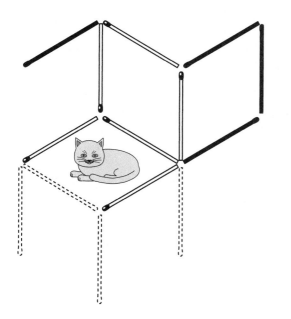

SQUARES IN THE WINDOW

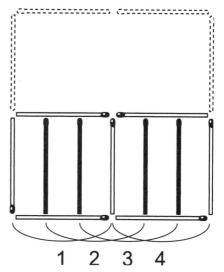

NOT ONE RHOMBUS
You need only remove three matchsticks as shown below.
Now it contains no rhombuses

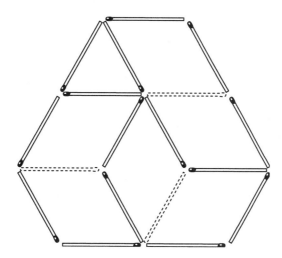

THE FLYING BIRD

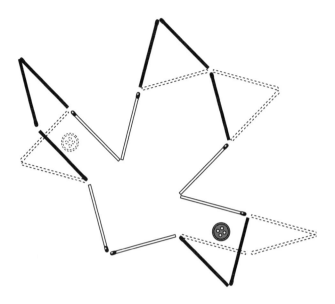

TWO MATCHING AREAS

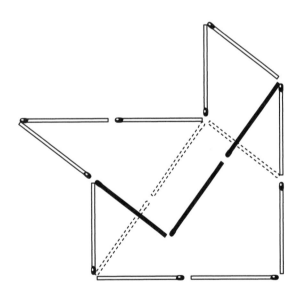

MATCH SIMILARITY

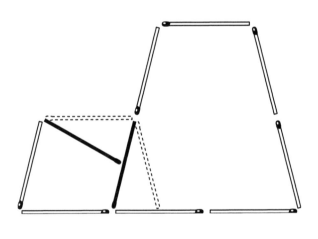

The New Puzzle Classics

SKEW RECTANGLE

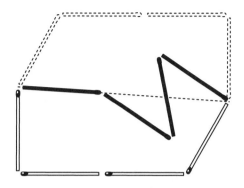

SQUARE & DIVISION

a

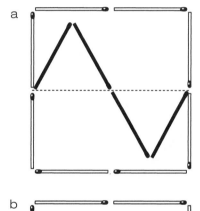

b

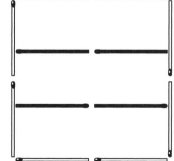

THE COTTAGE

a

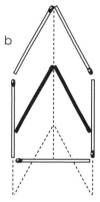

b

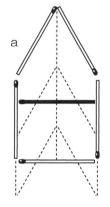

c

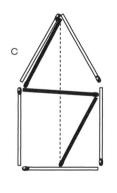

d

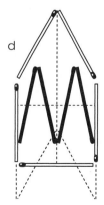

THE SHOE

THE MARQUEE

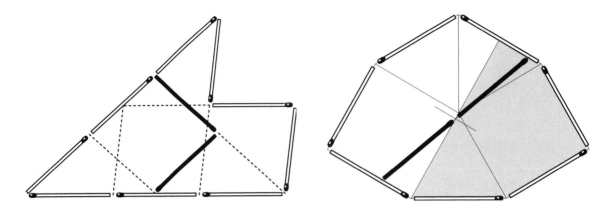

TRISECTION OF OCTAGON

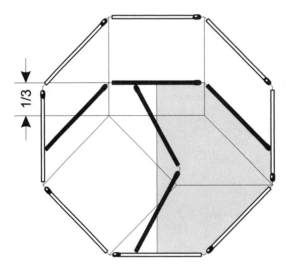

1/3

QUADRAGONAL

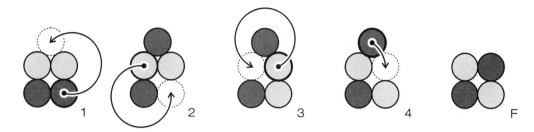

4 moves
Solution by SGJ

REDIRECT THE CORNER

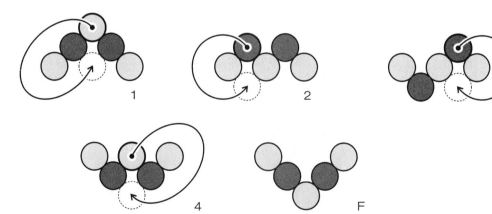

4 moves
Solution by SGJ

THE PENTA-COIN CHANGE

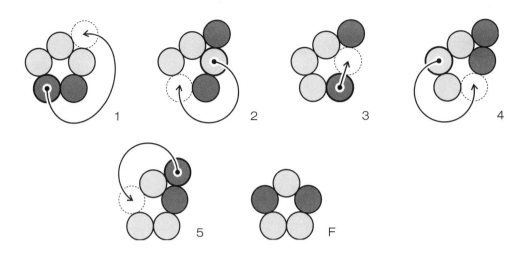

5 moves

TURN UP THE SHELL

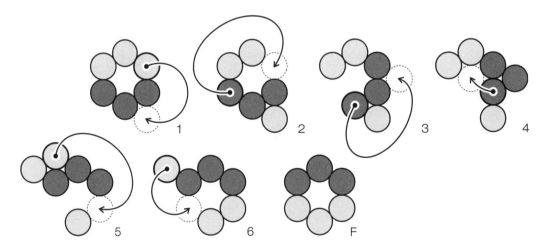

6 moves

The New Puzzle Classics

VERTICAL FLIP-FLOP

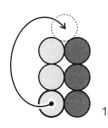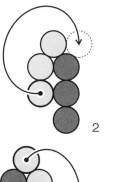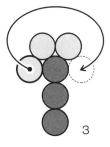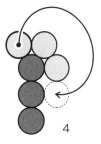

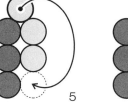

5 moves

SLIDE THE ROW

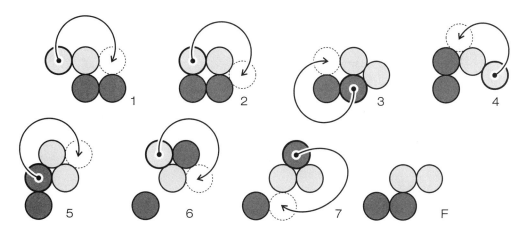

7 moves

THE T-COIN CHALLENGE

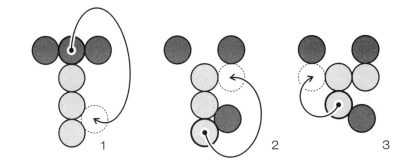

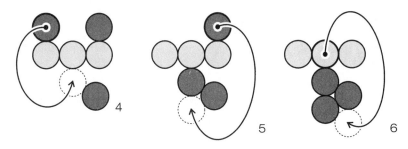

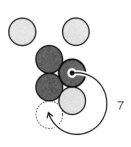

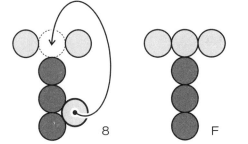

8 moves

HEXA-FLOWER

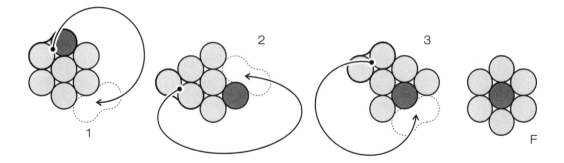

3 moves
Solution by SGJ

CHANGE COIN ROWS

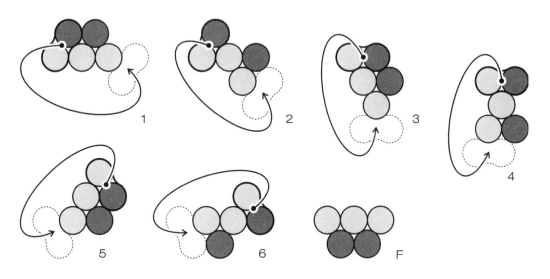

6 moves
Solution by SGJ

TRIADS

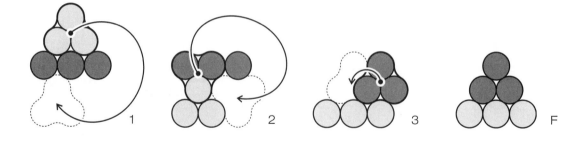

3 moves

TWELVE ROWS OF COINS

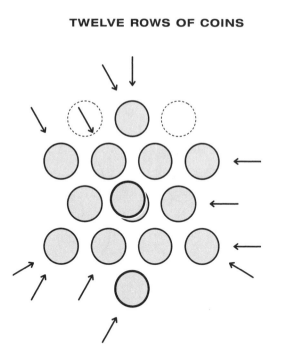

FOUR COIN SQUARES

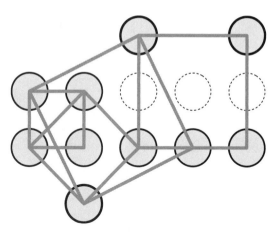

Witty Patterns—Solutions

THE WAFFLE PUZZLE

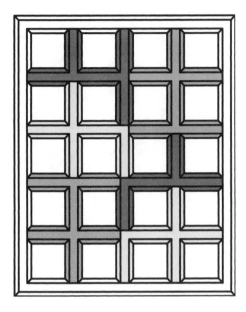

FOUR ARROWS

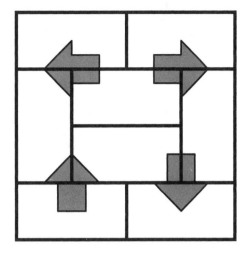

CHECKERED RECTANGLES

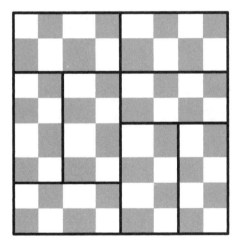

THE TANGRAMMED CHECKERBOARD

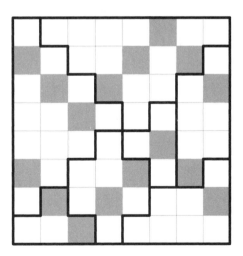

SQUARED COLOR SPOTS

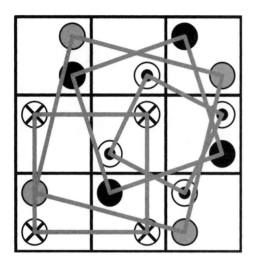

TETRA-MARBLES

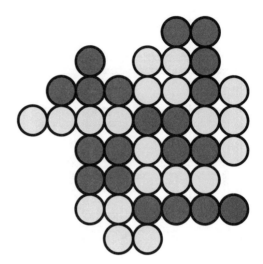

THE BERMUDA PEARLS

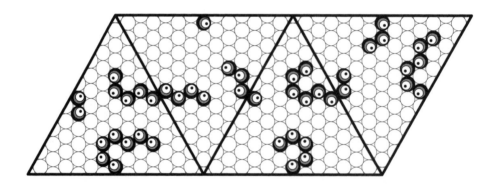

The New Puzzle Classics

THE MOLECULAR CHAIN PUZZLE

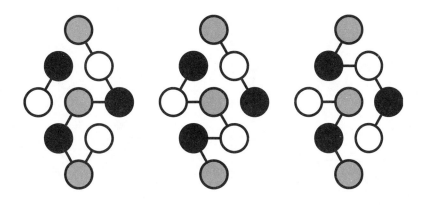

HEXA THREE-BY-THREE

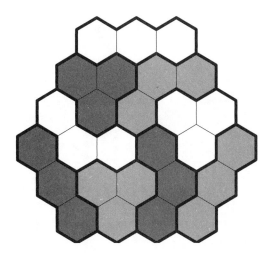

THE TRI-HEX PUZZLE

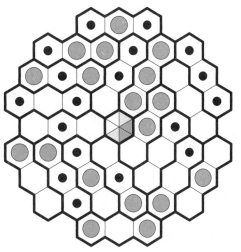

DISTORTED PENTASHAPES

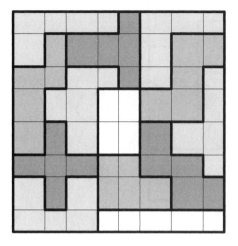

THE NINE BAT-SQUARES

TOUCH-ME-NOT BLOCKS

CHECKERED DOMINOES

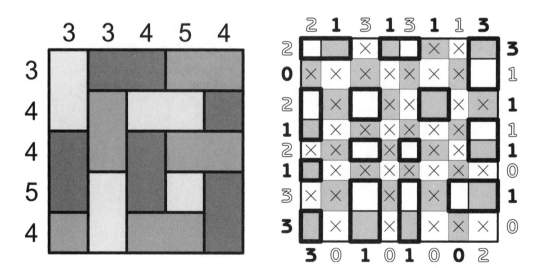

The New Puzzle Classics

THE PUZZLE PARK

THE CHECKERED TANGRAM: DOG, FOX, GOOSE & CORN

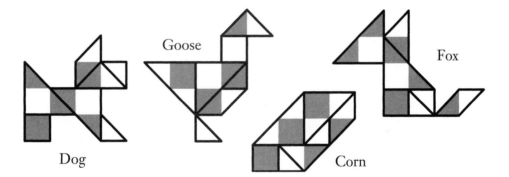

Goose

Fox

Dog

Corn

The way to get the whole company across the river is shown below:

```
M-D-G-F-C  =_=_=>  ***********************  ---------
D-G-C ---  **********  =M=F=>  ***********  ---------
D-G-C ---  **********  <=M=_=  ***********  F --------
D-G -----  **********  =M=C=>  ***********  F --------
D-G -----  **********  <=M=_=  ***********  C-F ------
G -------  **********  =M=D=>  ***********  C-F ------
G -------  **********  <=M=F=  ***********  D-C ------
F -------  **********  =M=G=>  ***********  D-C ------
F -------  **********  <=M=_=  ***********  G-D-C ----
---------  **********  =M=F=>  ***********  G-D-C ----
---------  ***********************  =_=_=>  M-F-G-D-C
```

WRAP THE BOX

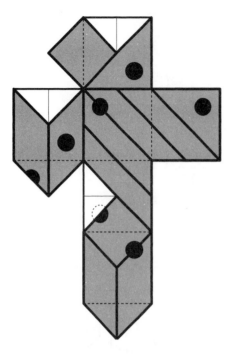

Solution by Peter Grabarchuk

THE HEXA-SPIRAL PATH PUZZLE

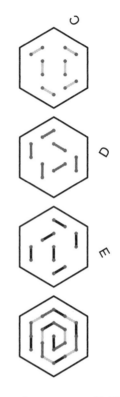

The three hexagons—C, D, and E—as they are shown above form the hexa-spiral path.

THE COLOR GRAINS PUZZLE

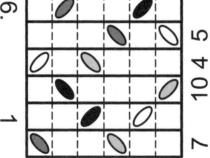

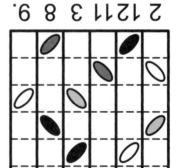

Inseparable groups of rings (shown in dark) in the patterns are made as follows:

Pattern A. Inseparable rings—a and c; separate ones—b and d.

Pattern B. Inseparable rings—a, b, c, and d.

Pattern C. Separate rings—a, b, c, and d.

Pattern D. Inseparable rings—a, b, and d; separate one—c.

Inseparable groups of rings in patterns B and D make remarkable mathematical objects called "Brunnian Links." These are topological objects consisting of several linked rings, which remain fully inseparable until any(!) one of them is removed. Then the remaining rings become fully separate. Specifically, the inseparable three-ring group in pattern D is well known as "Borromean Rings."

QUADRANGLES

In the star-like pattern it is possible to find sixty-two quadrangles of all shapes and sizes, both convex and concave. The pattern also contains thirty-two triangles of all possible sizes. All these shapes are shown in diagrams Q and T, respectively. Numbers next to every diagram show how many copies of the shape presented in this diagram are hidden in the pattern.

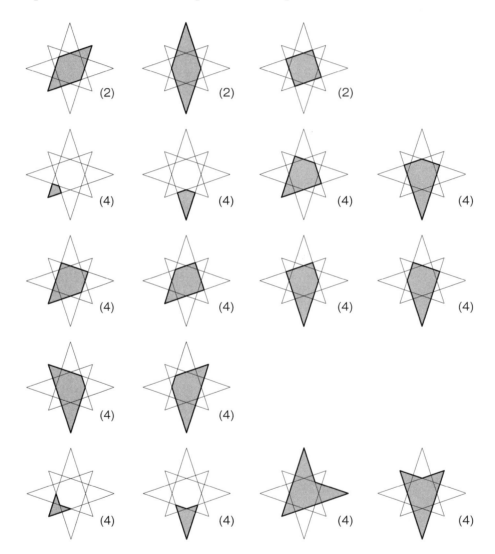

Figure Q. Sixty-two quadrangles hidden in the eight-pointed star.

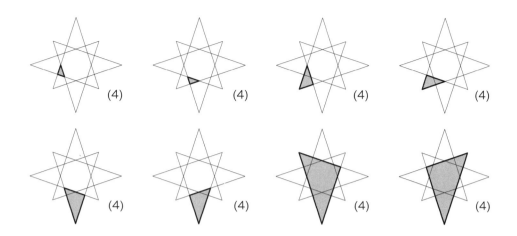

Figure T. Thirty-two triangles hidden in the eight-pointed star.

HOW MANY CANDIES?

In the big, candy-like grid it is possible to find seventy-three candies of all shapes and sizes, shown below. Numbers next to each candy show how many copies of that candy are hidden in the big grid.

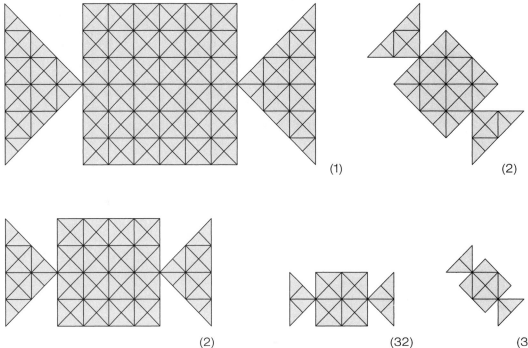

(1)

(2)

(2)

(32)

(36)

The New Puzzle Classics

THE TIME PICTOSCOPE

Each of the ancient symbols is composed of a letter rotated 90 degrees clockwise and its mirror image placed symmetrically to it. Since all but one were formed from among the first letters of the English alphabet, the remaining one is the I, and the ninth symbol is shown in the middle screen.

This puzzle was inspired by Martin Gardner's similar puzzle with digits.

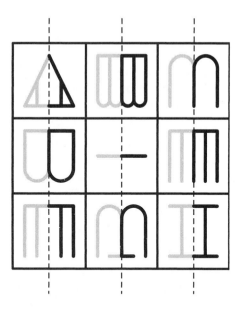

THE FIELD OF HEARTS CHALLENGE

The pair of exactly identical hearts is shown in the dark squares.

Words & Numbers—Solutions

TEST-FEST

The letter that should be placed in the circle with a question mark is the light N shown on the right. The letters in this chain are the initial letters of the sequence 2, 3, 4, ..., and so on, where shaded letters refer to even numbers and light letters are odd numbers, as shown in the right column below.

Nine

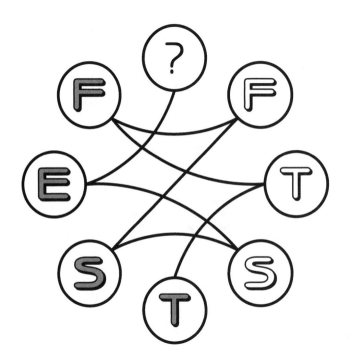

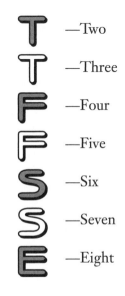

—Two

—Three

—Four

—Five

—Six

—Seven

—Eight

THE O-O-O-O PUZZLE

If you read from right to left beginning from the bottom and going to the top as shown with arrows 1 through 7 in the illustration below, the following well-known sentence will appear:

TO BE OR NOT TO BE?
It is obvious that the question mark should remain.

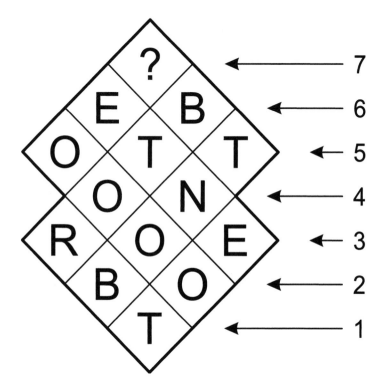

This puzzle is designed so that it is possible to fill in empty boxes both in the normal position of the whole word tower (diagram A), and in its upside-down orientation (diagram B). The difference is that only in the latter position can you get fifteen complete words. How this can be done is shown in diagram C.

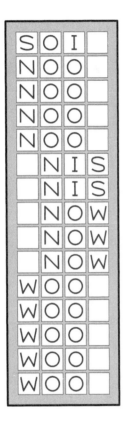

A

B

C

If we select from the English alphabet the 1st, 3rd, 5th, . . . , 23rd, and 25th letters we will have the following set: A, C, E, G, I, K, M, O, Q, S, U, W, and Y. All the words in the first line consist only of the letters chosen from this set.

Selecting the 1st, 4th, 7th, 10th, 13th, 16th, 19th, 22nd, and 25th letters, we have the following set: A, D, G, J, M, P, S, V, and Y. The words in the second line contain only letters from this set.

Using a similar rule we can select the 1st, 5th, 9th, 13th, 17th, 21st, and 25th letters, yielding the third set: A, E, I, M, Q, U, and Y. The third line contains only letters from this set.

Finally, selecting the 1st, 6th, 11th, 16th, 21st, and 26th letters, we get the last set: A, F, K, P, U, and Z. The two-letter word in the fourth line is made up using two letters taken from this set.

WE SAW WISE WACKO
AS DAY SPAM
MY AIM
UP

Letters distributed within the 5 X 5 square have different properties and can be organized into five different groups containing five letters each. Within every group, all letters share the same property. All five groups are shown in table A. As you can see, the outlines of the letters in Group 1 have no recognizable angles (of any value), while the letters in Group 2 have one angle each, in Group 3: two angles, in Group 4: three angles, and in Group 5 all letters have four angles each.

Now, fill in a 5 X 5 square with the angle numbers of the respective letters; we will get square B. Studying this number square, we can see that two of its rows and all of its columns contain different numbers 0 through 4, while the remaining rows, and two main diagonals are close to sharing the same property, but not quite. To make all of them contain different numbers, too, we need to swap just two pairs of numbers, 0-1 and 3-4, shown within two ovals, respectively. The mathematical object we get is called a Latin Square.

Finally, we can say that the rule that was applied to distribute the letters within the initial square is the Latin Square rule, or placing letters with different numbers of angles in every row, column, and every main diagonal. Thus, to restore the initial letter square, we should swap pairs U-L and K-E, respectively, as shown in square C.

No Angles	C J O S U
1 Angle	G L P R V
2 Angles	B D N T Z
3 Angles	F K M W Y
4 Angles	E H I Q X

A

The New Puzzle Classics

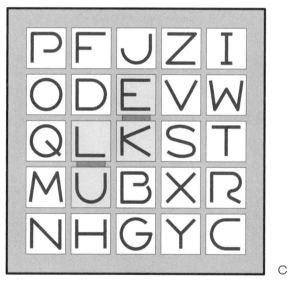

B

C

THE QUICK PUZZLE

In the picture on the right you can recognize three stylized capital letters— A, X, and U. At the same time, these letters form the image of an opened envelope with a piece of paper inside it. Under the envelope you can see two more envelopes. So the picture means: "three letters."

THE FOXY BOX

Move a matchstick as shown in diagram A below, and then turn the whole word 90 degrees clockwise. You will read the "fox" from top to bottom as shown in diagram B at right.

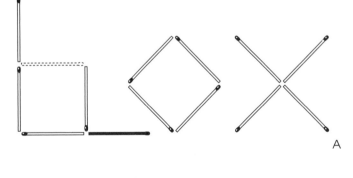

A

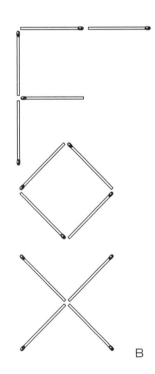

B

Reassemble the pieces of the word "mice" (illustration A) as shown in illustration B. Now you can read (from top to bottom) the word "cat" composed of the light letters C, A, and T of the same height, which are placed in a straight line, and do not touch one another.

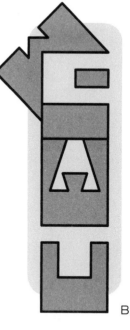

A

B

ONE SQUARE

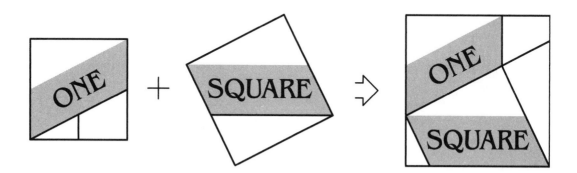

MOON & STAR

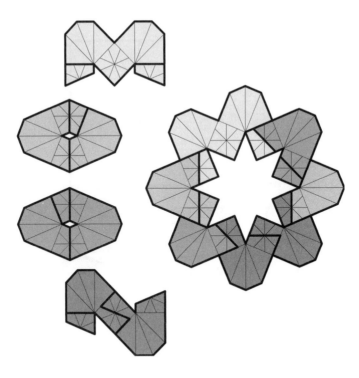

THE CHALLENGE OF THE WALL MAZE

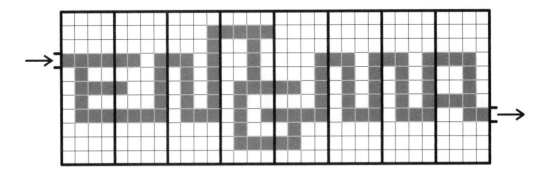

The message consists of a single word—"enigma."

HARD AS XYZ

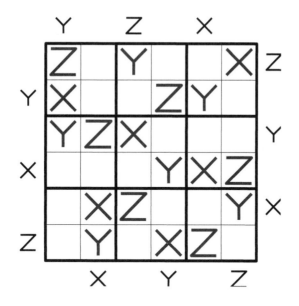

IF & THEN

Every equation computes so that its sum equals the total number of all recognizable angles (of any value) in the shapes of the digits of the addends. The digits with all their angles are shown in the illustration on the right. So the number to replace the question mark in the last sentence is 7.

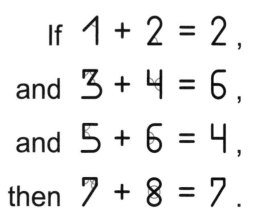

If $1 + 2 = 2$,

and $3 + 4 = 6$,

and $5 + 6 = 4$,

then $7 + 8 = 7$.

PUZZLER'S MERRY-GO-ROUND

123+4+5+6+7+8-9-1+0+111x2=365

4 - 3 =

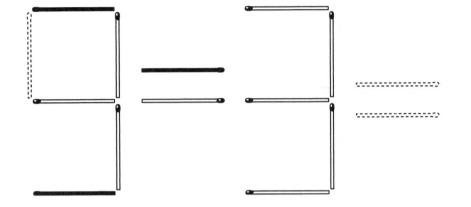

THE PUZZLE OF THE "VII"

THE X-SYMMETRY CHALLENGE

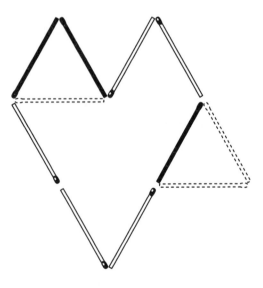

You can see four ✕ s.

HEXA SIX

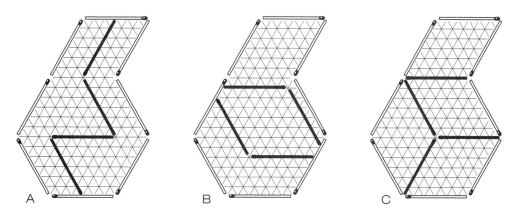

MAGIC 3 X 3 DISSECTION

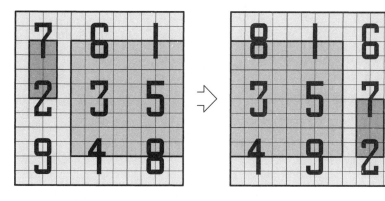

Solution 1

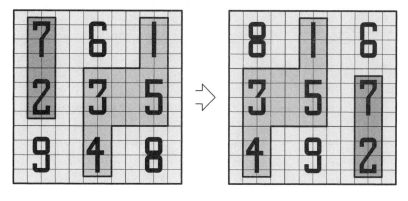

Solution 2—by Vladimir Rybinskiy

THE EIGHT-INTO-ZERO CHANGE

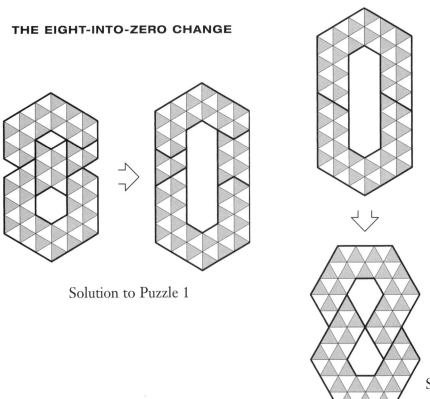

Solution to Puzzle 1

Solution to
Puzzle 2

THE ZERO-INFINITY MYSTERY

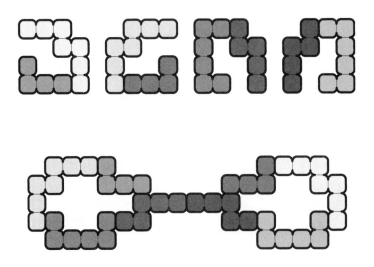

The New Puzzle Classics

INVISIBLE DIGITAL TILING

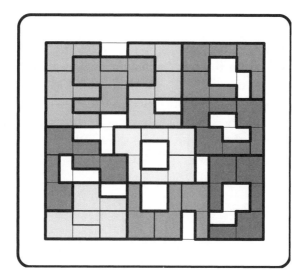

THE WIRE COUNT

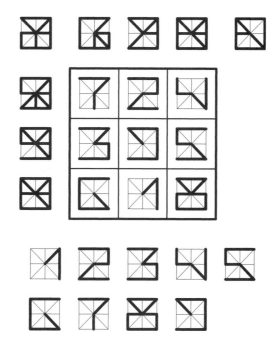

Turn the whole maze 180 degrees as shown in diagrams A and B below. Now, starting from the 1 (in diagram B) go to the maze's exit. You will get the following sequence: 1 2 ? 8 1 6. You can see that it consists of the numbers 1, 2, . . . , 8, 16 which shows that the 4 is the number to replace the question mark.

The final maze sequence is presented in diagram C. Note that it does not matter whether you replace the question mark with the 4 before or after you rotate the maze. The 4, like several other digits, has rotational symmetry, and so it looks the same either right-side up or upside-down.

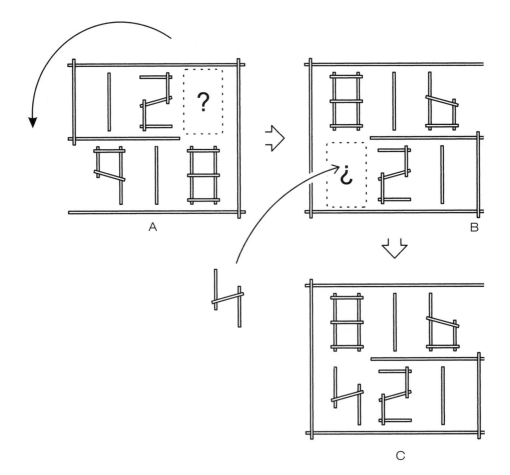

Origami Puzzles—Solutions

FOLD TWO TO THREE

Fold both origami squares as shown in diagrams 1 and 2. Then join them as shown in diagram M, and you will obtain the shape F, in which you can see three squares—one smaller (as shaded in the middle of the shape) and two bigger ones around it.

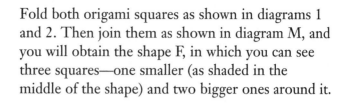

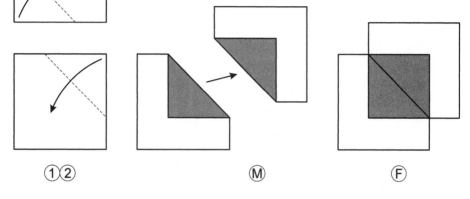

THREE-INTO-ONE FOLDS

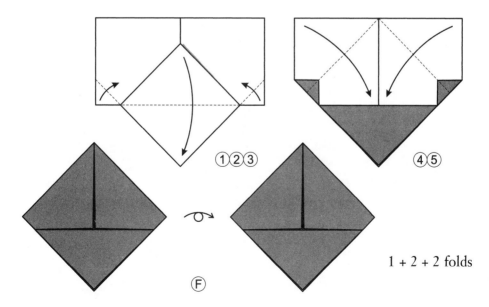

1 + 2 + 2 folds

THE ORIGAMI MINI-DOMINOES

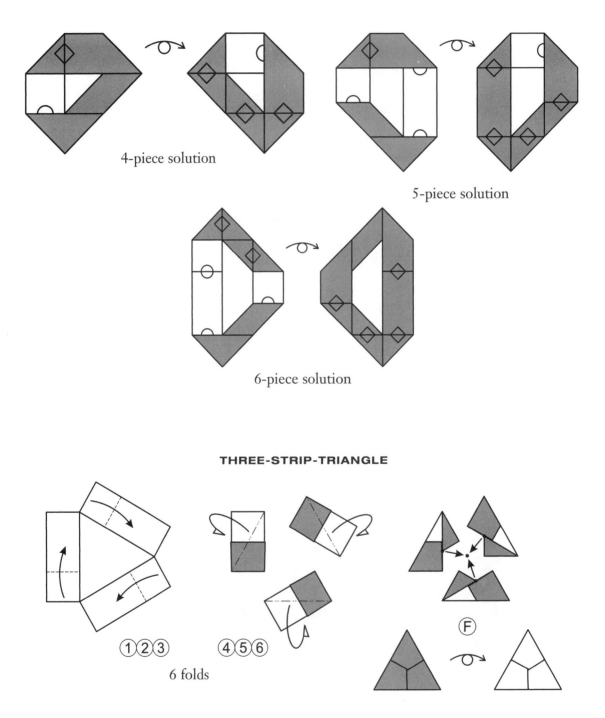

4-piece solution

5-piece solution

6-piece solution

THREE-STRIP-TRIANGLE

①②③   ④⑤⑥

6 folds

F

THE WOVEN COLORED SQUARE

The whole process of interweaving the four puzzle pieces into a square packet is shown in steps 1 through 19. The final result is presented in the diagram F. In interweaving the pieces, keep in mind that every step has to be performed in a "symmetric" way; that is, the back side (visible and internal layers) of the assem-bling packet you are manipulating must be an exact mirror image of its face at all times. Three diagrams of step 4 illustrate this well. As you can see diagrams 4a and 4c show the face side of the building packet, while diagram 4b shows its back.

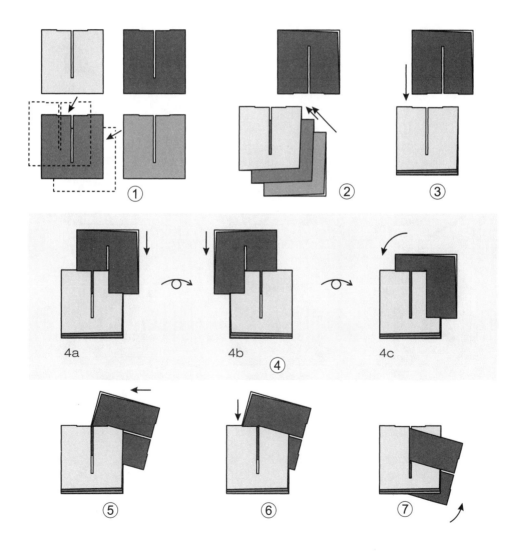

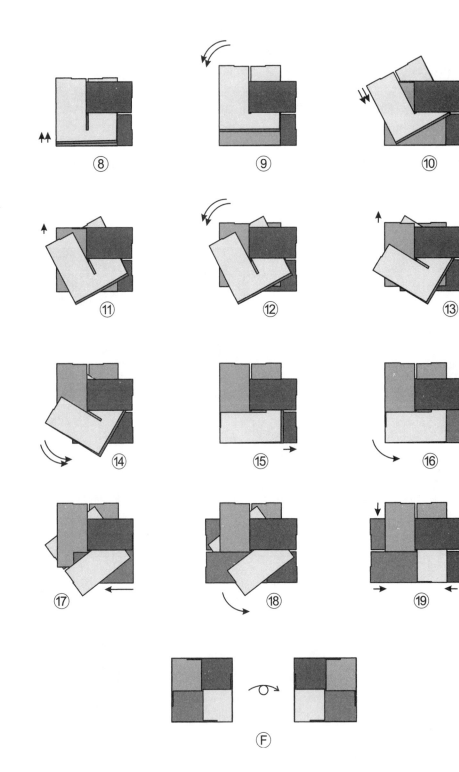

⑧

⑨

⑩

⑪

⑫

⑬

⑭

⑮

⑯

⑰

⑱

⑲

Ⓕ

THE STAR OF ORIGAMI

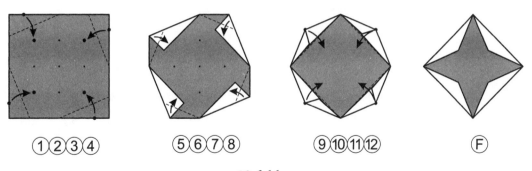

①②③④ ⑤⑥⑦⑧ ⑨⑩⑪⑫ Ⓕ

12 folds

THE CHECKERED ORIGAMI TRIMINO

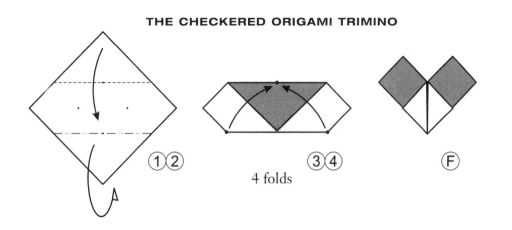

①② ③④ Ⓕ

4 folds

SKEW TRIMINO PATTERN

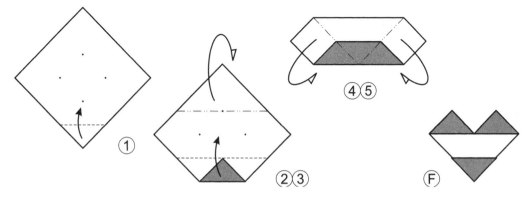

① ②③ ④⑤ Ⓕ

5 folds

THE ORIGAMI CHECKERBOARD PUZZLE (SOLUTION 1)

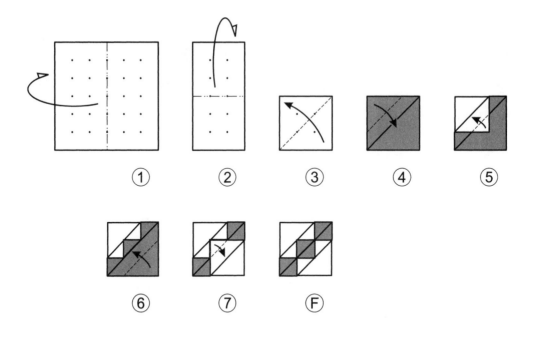

7 folds

THE ORIGAMI CHECKERBOARD PUZZLE (SOLUTION 2)

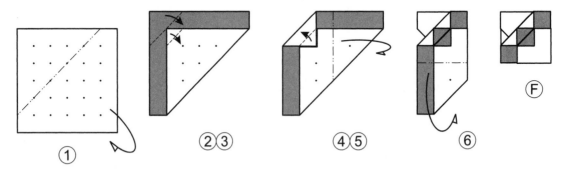

6 folds

THE ORIGAMI CHECKERBOARD PUZZLE (SOLUTION 3)

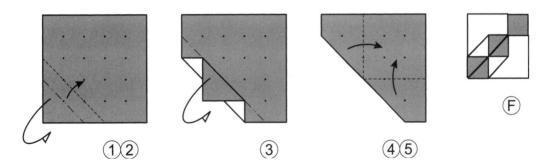

①②   ③   ④⑤   Ⓕ

5 folds
Solution by Koji Kitajima and Hiroshi Yamamoto

THE ORIGAMI PROPELLER

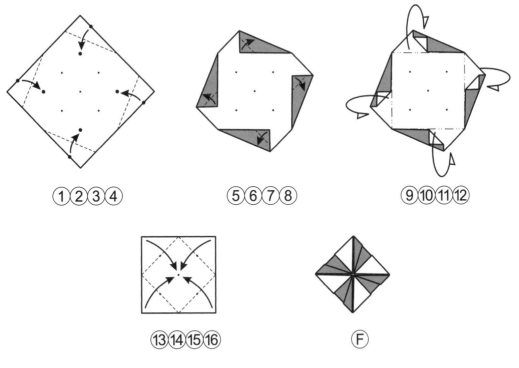

①②③④   ⑤⑥⑦⑧   ⑨⑩⑪⑫

⑬⑭⑮⑯   Ⓕ

16 folds

THE ORIGAMI HOUSE PUZZLE

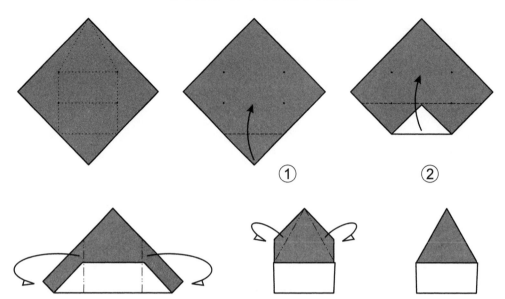

6 folds

THE ORIGAMI GREEK CROSS

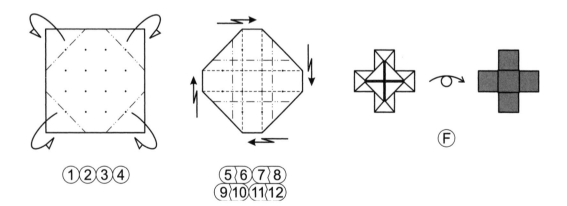

12 folds

THE ORIGAMI DOMINO

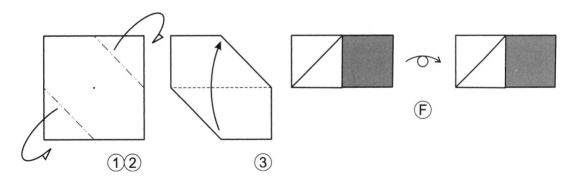

①② ③ Ⓕ

3 folds
Solution by Peter Grabarchuk

THE CHECKERED TRIMINO

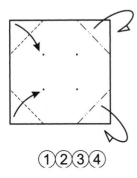 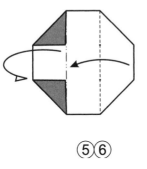 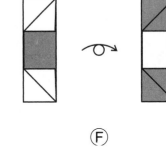

①②③④ ⑤⑥ Ⓕ

6 folds

TRIANGLE-IN-RECTANGLE

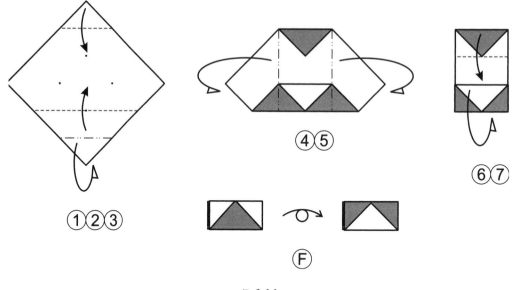

① ② ③

④ ⑤

⑥ ⑦

Ⓕ

7 folds

SKEW DOMINO PATTERN

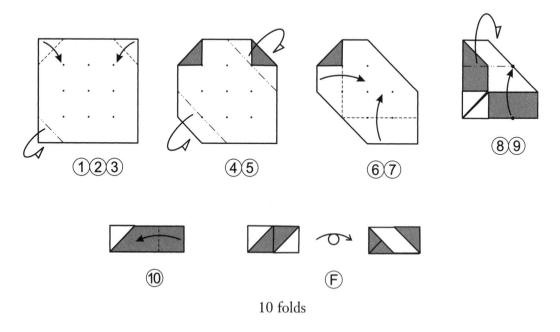

① ② ③

④ ⑤

⑥ ⑦

⑧ ⑨

⑩

Ⓕ

10 folds

THE ORIGAMI HILL

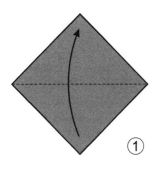

①

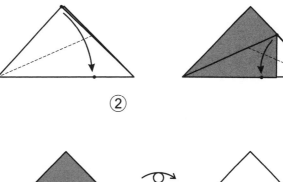

②

③

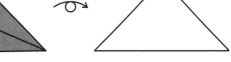

F

3 folds

TWO SIDES OF THE MOUNTAIN

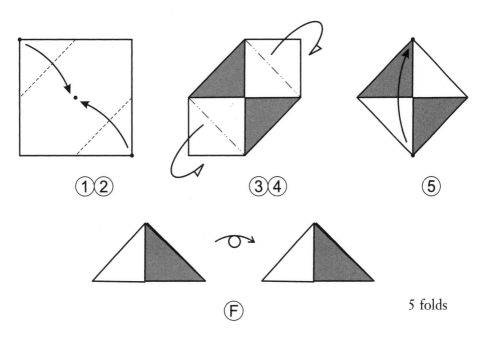

①②

③④

⑤

F

5 folds

THE MOUNTAIN SEASONS

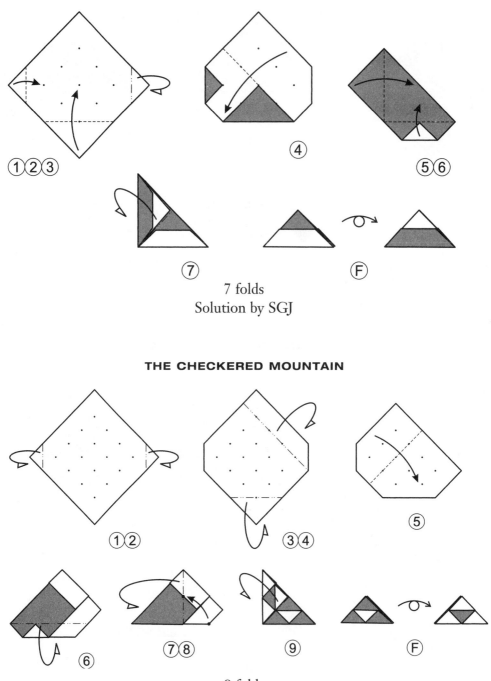

① ② ③

④

⑤ ⑥

⑦

Ⓕ

7 folds
Solution by SGJ

THE CHECKERED MOUNTAIN

① ②

③ ④

⑤

⑥

⑦ ⑧

⑨

Ⓕ

9 folds

LAKE & MOUNTAIN

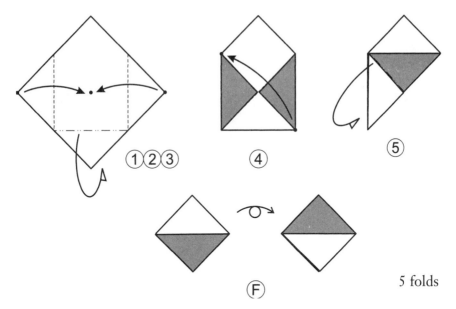

①②③   ④   ⑤

Ⓕ   5 folds

THE LITTLE ORIGAMI CHESSBOARD

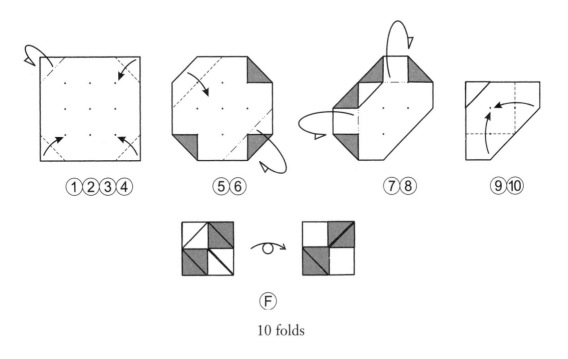

①②③④   ⑤⑥   ⑦⑧   ⑨⑩

Ⓕ

10 folds

Solutions   **309**

DIAGONAL CRISSCROSS

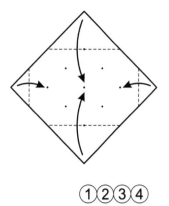

①②③④

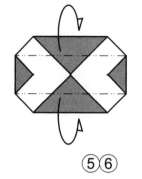

⑤⑥

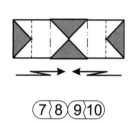

⑦⑧⑨⑩

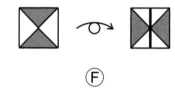

Ⓕ

10 folds

THE ORIGAMI WINDOW

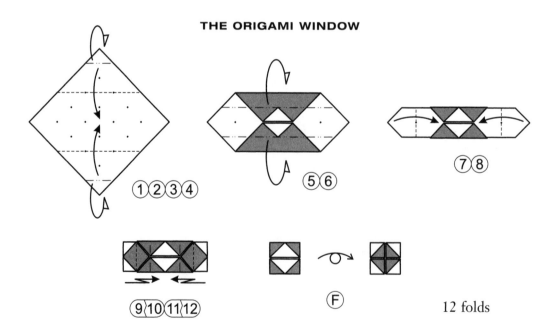

①②③④

⑤⑥

⑦⑧

⑨⑩⑪⑫

Ⓕ

12 folds

Tricky Moves—Solutions

CHANGE THE LEVELS

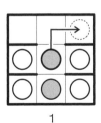

1

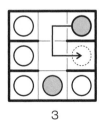

2

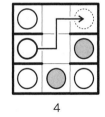

3

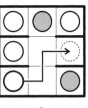

4

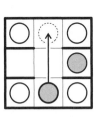

5

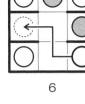

6

7

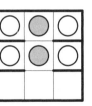

8

9

F

9 moves
Solution by SGJ

MOVES IN THE H

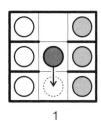 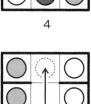 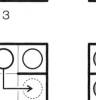

| 1 | 2 | 3 | 4 |

 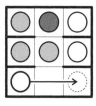 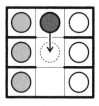

| 5 | 6 | 7 | 8 |

| 9 | 10 | 11 | 12 |

| F |

12 moves
Solution by SGJ

CHANGE THE COLUMNS

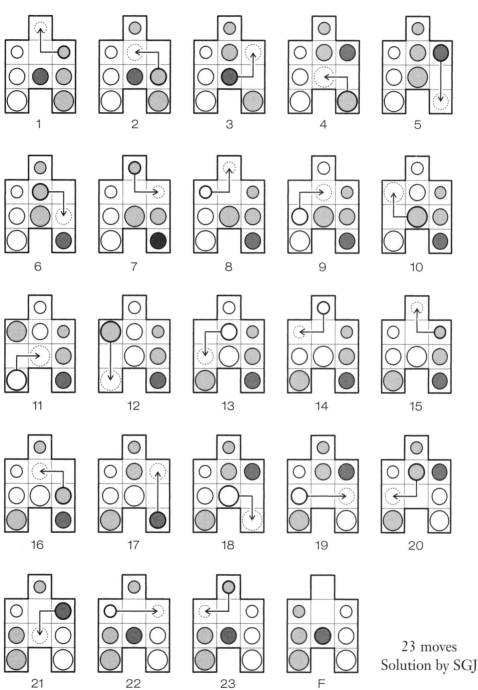

23 moves
Solution by SGJ

THE SPIRAL GALAXY MYSTERY

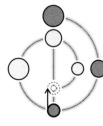

1

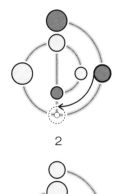

2

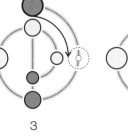

3

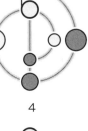

4

5

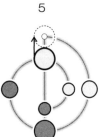

6

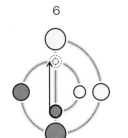

7

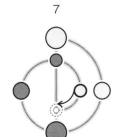

8

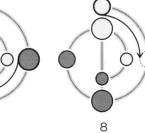

9

10

11

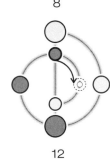

12

13

14

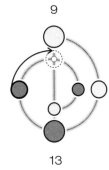

15

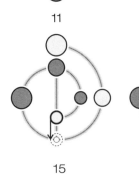

F

15 moves
Solution by SGJ

BEES & LADYBUGS

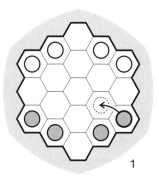

1

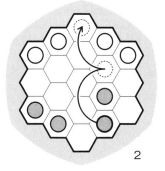

2

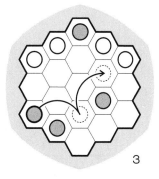

3

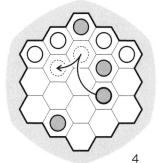

4

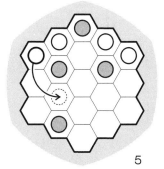

5

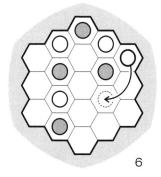

6

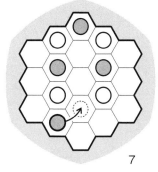

7

F

7 moves
Solution by SGJ

THE BIG BEE CHALLENGE

19 moves
Solution by SGJ

HEXAGONAL CRISSCROSS

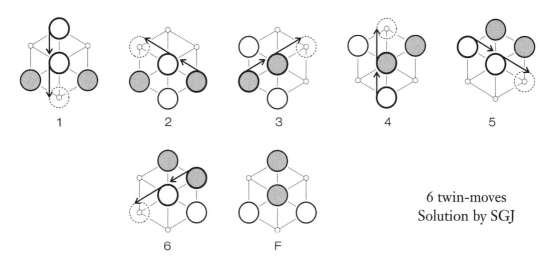

1   2   3   4   5

6   F

6 twin-moves
Solution by SGJ

THE FRAMED MOVE CHALLENGE

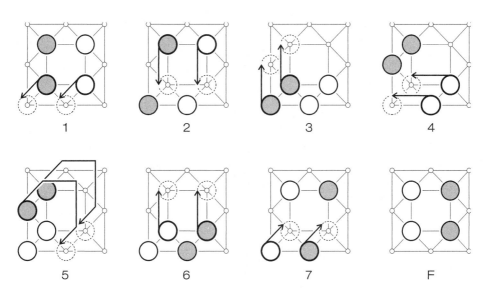

1   2   3   4

5   6   7   F

7 twin-moves
Solution by SGJ

CHALLENGING HOPSCOTCH

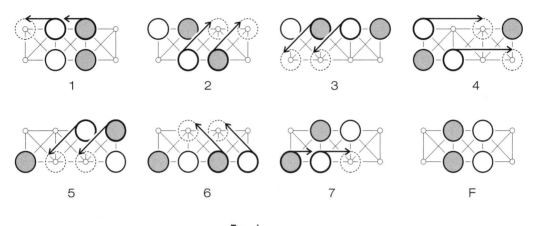

1   2   3   4

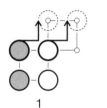 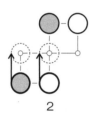 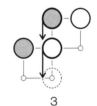 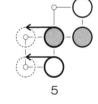

5   6   7   F

7 twin-moves
Solution by SGJ

TWO JOINED SQUARES

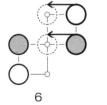 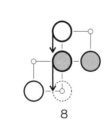 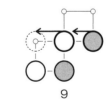

1   2   3   4   5

6   7   8   9   F

9 twin-moves

SPINNING PUZZLE

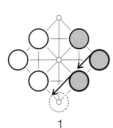

1

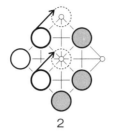

2

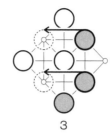

3

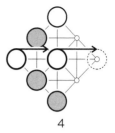

4

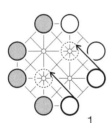

5

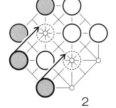

6

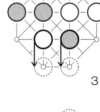

F

6 twin-moves
Solution by SGJ

EIGHT COUNTERS IN OCTAGON

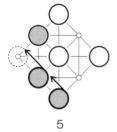

1

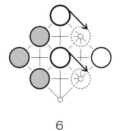

2

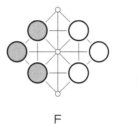

3

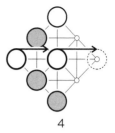

4

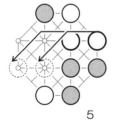

5

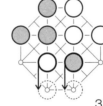

6

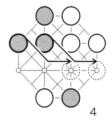

7

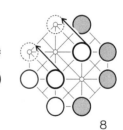

8

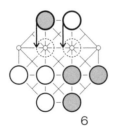

F

8 twin-moves

Solutions

319

HEXA X-CHANGES

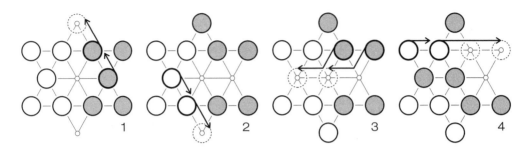

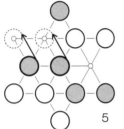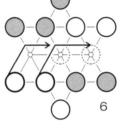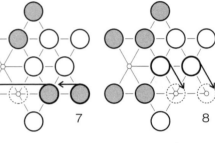

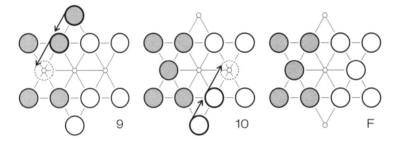

10 twin-moves
Solution by SGJ

The New Puzzle Classics

SQUARE REARRANGEMENT

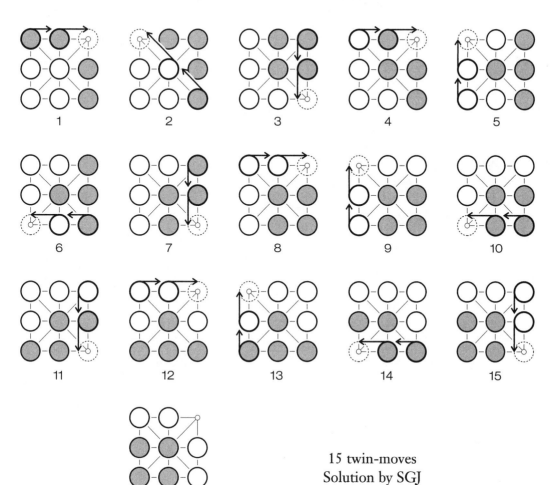

15 twin-moves
Solution by SGJ

DRUMMING MOVES

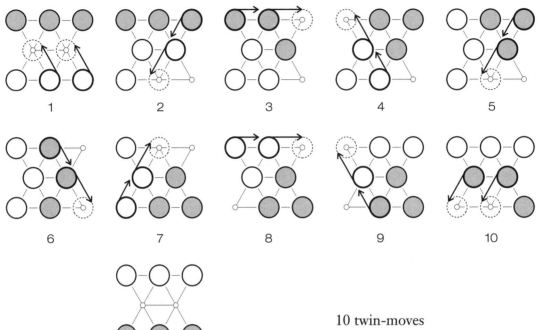

1 2 3 4 5

6 7 8 9 10

F

10 twin-moves
Solution by SGJ

The New Puzzle Classics

THE ANCIENT BUTTERFLY

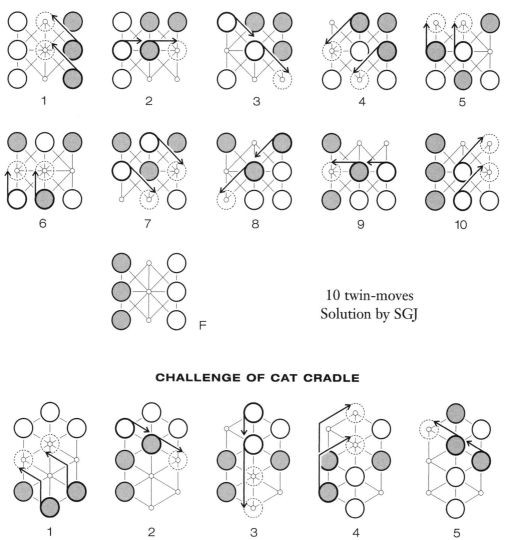

10 twin-moves
Solution by SGJ

CHALLENGE OF CAT CRADLE

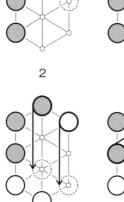
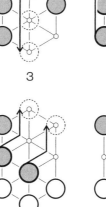
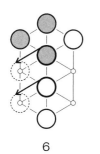
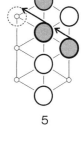

8 twin-moves
Solution by SGJ

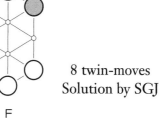

THE FISHBONE PUZZLE

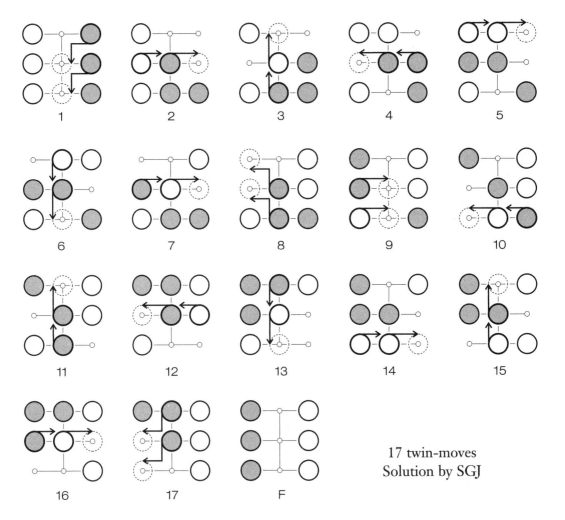

17 twin-moves
Solution by SGJ

THE KNIGHT MAZE

To exchange the knights you will need eighteen single leaps, as shown below.

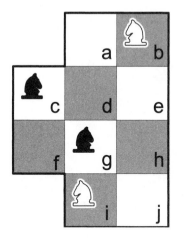

1. c - h.	11. c - b.
2. h - a.	12. b - g.
3. a - f.	13. h - c.
4. b - c.	14. c - b.
5. c - h.	15. a - h.
6. h - a.	16. h - c.
7. g - b.	17. f - e.
8. b - c.	18. e - i.
9. c - h.	
10. i - c.	18 leaps

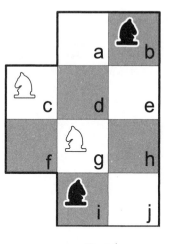

Start   Finish

KNIGHT'S MANEUVERS

Seven moves to get from the start to the final position are as follows:

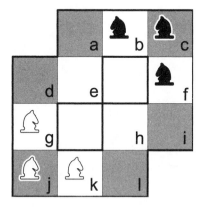

1. k - i.
2. c - h - d - k.
3. g - a - h - c.
4. b - d - h - a - g.
5. j - h - d - b.
6. f - a - h - j.
7. i - e - l - f.

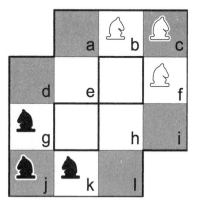

Start   7 moves   Finish
Solution by SGJ

KNIGHT-ROOK EXCHANGE

To swap the lines of knights and rooks you will need to perform
eight moves as shown below.

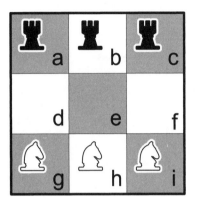

1. R (c - f).
2. Kn (h - c).
3. R (b - e - h).
4. Kn (i - b).
5. R (f - i).
6. Kn (g - f).
7. R (a - d - g).
8. Kn (f - a).

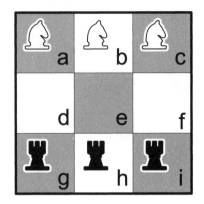

Start

8 moves
Solution by SGJ

Finish

ALL THE KING'S MEN

You can "turn" the whole position 180 degrees in ten moves shown below.
Actually, according to chess rules, the pawn moves forward only; thus,
in this puzzle it must always remain at its starting cell.

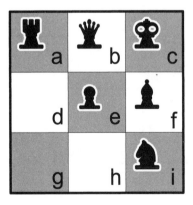

1. R (a - d - g - h).
2. Q (b - d - g).
3. K (c - b).
4. Kn (i - d - c).
5. R (h - i).
6. K (b - d).
7. Kn (c - h - a).
8. Q (g - h).
9. K (d - g).
10. B (f - b - d).

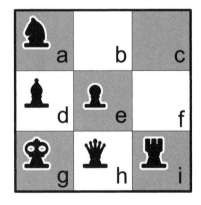

Start

10 moves
Solution by SGJ

Finish

The New Puzzle Classics

CROSS THE LAKE

To cross the lake, perform the fourteen moves shown below.

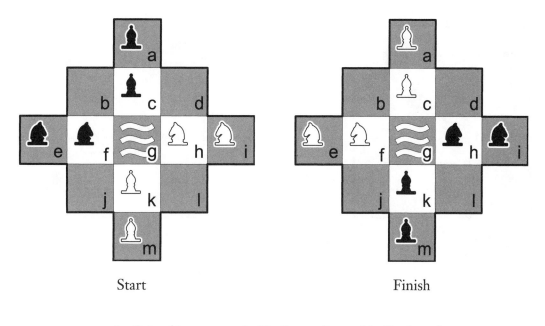

Start   Finish

1. B (a - b).   6. Kn (i - c - l).   11. Kn (m - f).
2. B (m - j).   7. Kn (e - c - i).   12. Kn (a - h).
3. Kn (f - a).   8. Kn (l - c - e).   13. B (b - l - m).
4. Kn (h - m).   9. B (k - f - c).   14. B (j - d - a).
5. B (c - h).   10. B (h - k).

                                             14 moves

CHANGE THE ROOKS

Twenty moves to change the rooks are shown below.

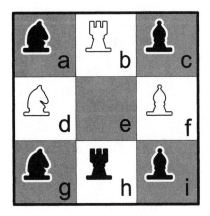

Start

1. B (i - e).
2. R (h - i).
3. Kn (a - h).
4. B (e - a).
5. B (c - e).
6. Kn (h - c).
7. R (i - h).
8. B (e - i).
9. R (h - e).
10. Kn (c - h).
11. Kn (d - c).
12. R (e - d).
13. B (a - e).
14. R (d - a).
15. Kn (c - d).
16. B (e - c).
17. R (b - e).
18. R (a - b).
19. Kn (h - a).
20. R (e - h).

20 moves
Solution by SGJ

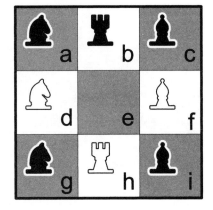

Finish

Challenging Mix—Solutions

THE FIVE Y'S

The placement of four and five Y's to form four equilateral triangles are shown in diagrams A and B, respectively.

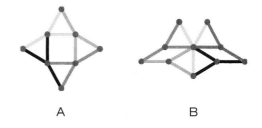

A   B

SIX WIRE CORNERS

Diagram A shows the solution to Puzzle 1 with three triangles and two squares. To solve Puzzle 2 and to form three squares, you have to go into the third dimension and build up an octahedron from the six wire corners as shown in diagram B. This gives you three squares that are situated within the octahedron as shown in illustration C; the squares are shaded.

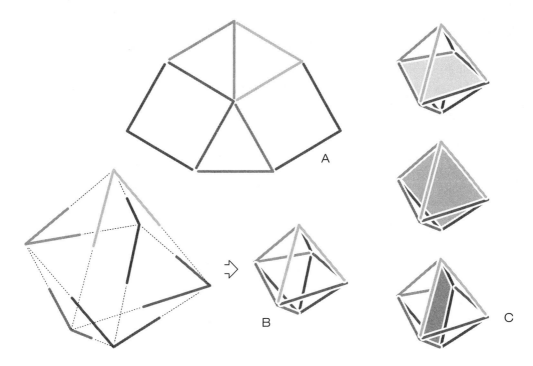

A

B

C

THE EIGHT STICK CHALLENGE

The fence of the minimal area inscribed exactly into a 9 X 9 square is shown in the diagram on the right. Its area totals 20 square units.

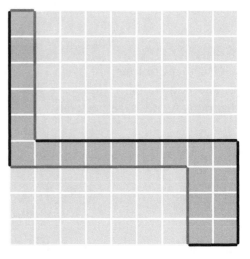

THE FENCE PUZZLE

The octagon on the left with sides 12, 8, 10, 9, 12 (11+1), 8 (2+6), 10 (3+7), 9 (4+5) has an area of about 456.46 square units; all angles of the octagon are 135 degrees.

The solution to the "no-180-degrees" variation is shown on the right, and gives the maximal result with an area of 449.39 square units. Both solutions by Nick Baxter. Try to find both minimal solutions on your own.

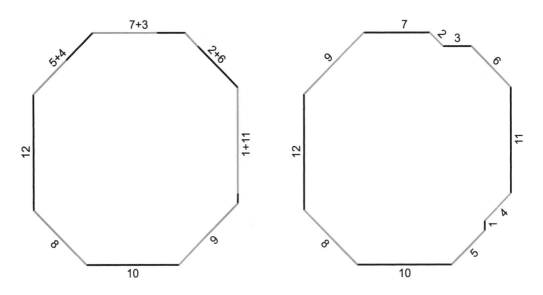

One degree-45 Snake-15 and its graph are shown in diagrams A and B, respectively. One degree-30 Snake-20 and its graph are presented in diagrams C and D, respectively.

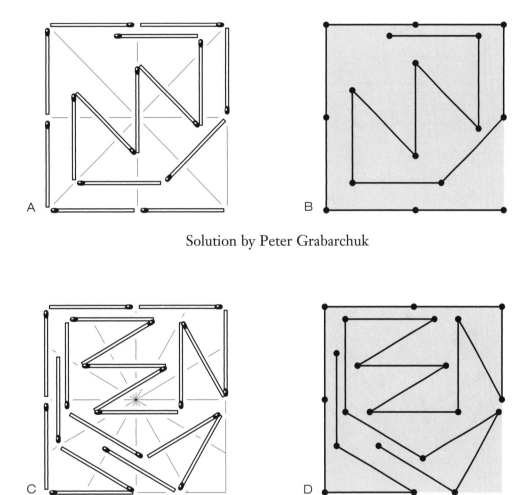

Solution by Peter Grabarchuk

Solution by Susan Hoover

The maximal known matchstick snakes of degree-30 for pentagon (Snake-6), hexagon (Snake-11), heptagon (Snake-14), and octagon (Snake-18) are shown in diagrams A, B, C, and D, respectively.

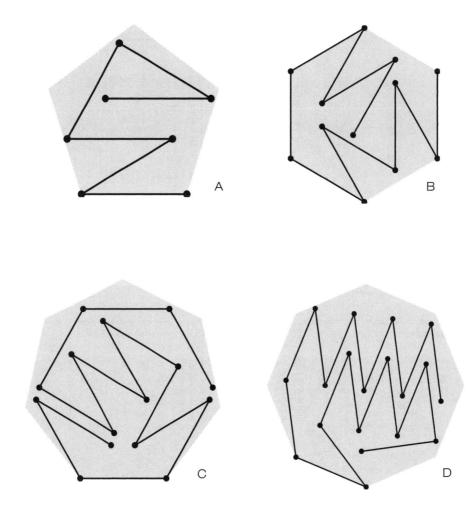

THE MATCHSTICK SNAKE IN A CIRCLE

The longest matchstick snake within a circle with a unit radius is a degree-30 Snake-12. Its graph is shown on the right.

Solution by Peter Grabarchuk

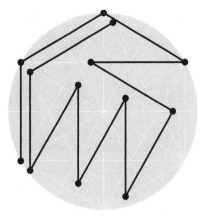

PLACE & TURN

It is possible to place twenty matchsticks onto the grid in the "place & turn" manner as shown in the diagrams below. Numbers and arrows in the diagrams show the order for placing matchsticks and the directions for their turns, respectively. Diagram A shows the position on the grid before the first turn, while diagram B shows the whole position before the last, twentieth turn.

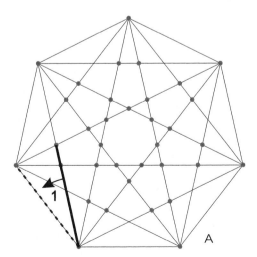

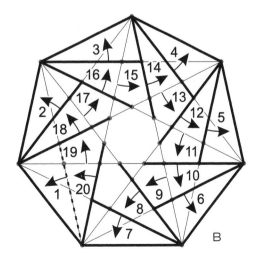

TWO WEAVING LOOPS

The whole rope pattern under a sheet of paper can be formed as shown below.

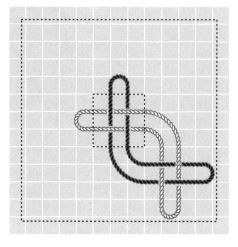

THE FENCED KNIGHT'S TOUR

The longest, seventeen-leap noncrossing knight's tour for a square boundary is shown below.

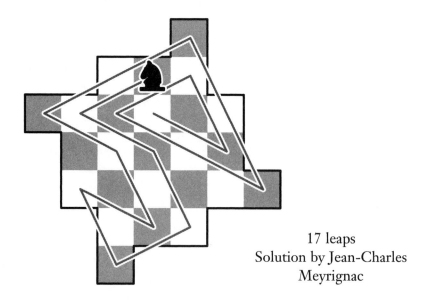

17 leaps
Solution by Jean-Charles
Meyrignac

THE RED TRIANGLE PUZZLE

Diagrams A and B below show how to put the three cubes together in order to form an equilateral triangle of the three bold (such as red) lines depicted on the cubes so that the final construction is stable when built on the table. Diagram C shows how the red triangle is situated within the construction of the three cubes.

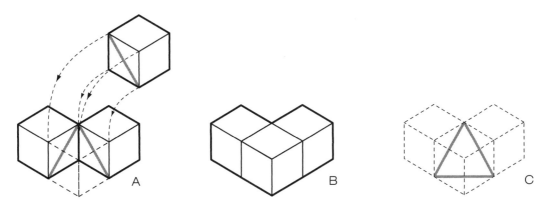

THE YELLOW CUBE PUZZLE

To build a yellow cube, place all the six cubes as shown in diagrams A and B. The final construction is stable when built on the table. Diagram C shows a yellow (shaded) cube as it is situated inside the construction of the six cubes.

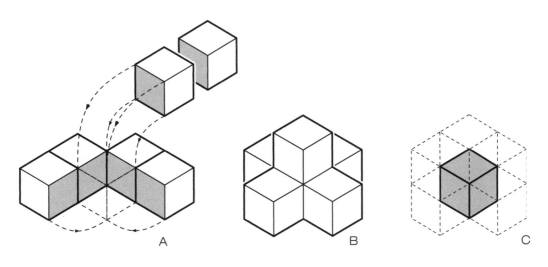

THE SOFTY CHALLENGE

The long 1 X 1 X 8 block squeezed into a 1 X 1 X 1 cube yields cube F.

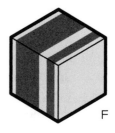

THE WOODEN PATTERNS PUZZLE

To get a cube with the same pattern on each of its six faces, you should orient it so that its main diagonal will coincide with the long axis of the log as shown in diagram A. Then make six cuts as shown in diagrams B and C, and you will get the cube shown in illustration D, which, in fact, shows just one face of the cube exactly as it was cut out. The full layout of the cube with six faces having the same pattern is shown in diagram E.

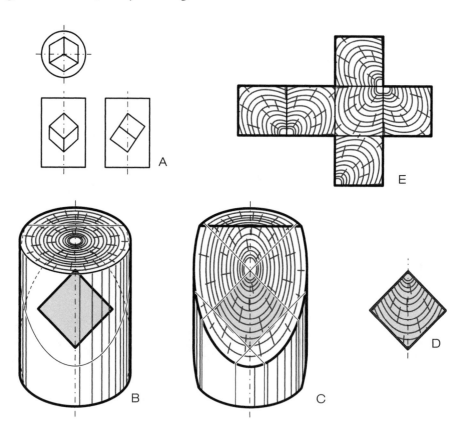

It is a well-known fact that if we join the middle points of the six edges of the cube as shown in diagram A we get a regular hexagon; it is shaded. Now inscribe a circle in this hexagon. It will form a base for a cone, and will have the largest possible diameter. This cone's vertex coincides with a corner of the cube, and its axis coincides with the longest diagonal of the cube, which connects its opposite corners as shown in diagram B. If we have a unit cube, with its edge 1, then the largest base of the cone has as its diameter the square root of (3/2), and its height is the square root of 3 divided by 2. As diagram C shows, two equal copies of the cone with the largest base and height can be placed symmetrically inside the cube.

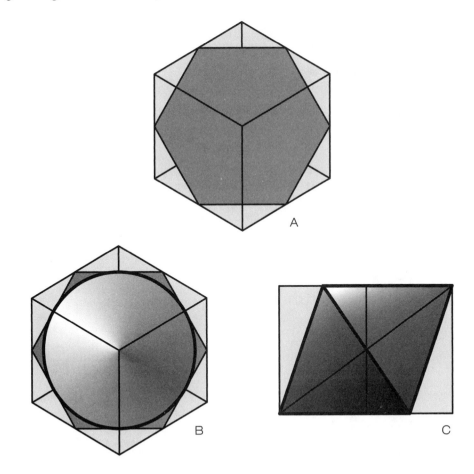

A

B

C

THE PLATE PACKING (4K-5I)

Both solutions are shown in illustrations A and B, respectively. Illustration A shows how four K-plates can fit inside a 1 X 1 X 1 cube. Illustration B shows how to put five I-plates inside a 1 X 1 X 1 cube. In the lowermost portion of each illustration you can see the complete set of the respective pieces. Above them you can see how every piece is situated within its respective cube.

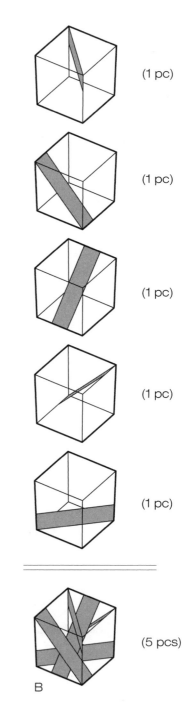

(1 pc)

(1 pc)

(1 pc)

(1 pc)

(1 pc)

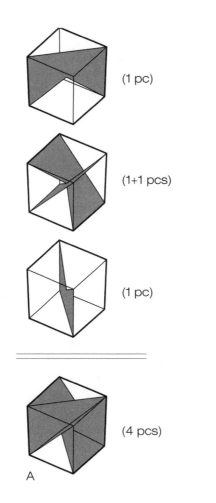

(1 pc)

(1+1 pcs)

(1 pc)

(4 pcs)

A

(5 pcs)

B

THE PAPER CUBE PUZZLE

If we cut all eight corners out of the initial cube as shown in illustration A, we will have four large pyramidal pieces that will form the large cube, B, and four small pyramidal pieces to assemble the small cube, D. Also, we cut six long rectangles obtained from the middle parts of the initial cube's faces into two smaller rectangles each. This way, we yield twelve rectangles that can form the medium-size cube, C.

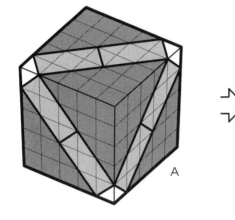

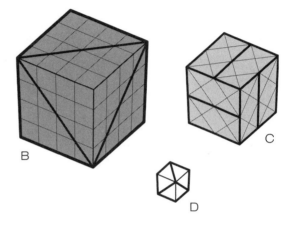

THE PAPER TETRAHEDRON PUZZLE

Divide a paper tetrahedron into eight pieces as shown in illustrations A and a. Four bigger pieces can now easily be paired up into two tetrahedrons, B and C, as shown in illustrations b and c. Four small equilateral triangles form a small tetrahedron, D (see illustration d).

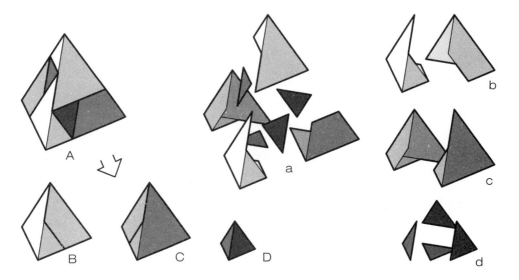

TWO SIMILAR TUBES

Illustrations A, B, C, and D show how to divide a 2 X 2 X 5 paper tube into four parts that can make two new tubes similar to each other. These are 1 X 1 X 2 and 2 X 2 X 4 tubes, which are similar, since their respective dimensions are at the same ratio—1:2.

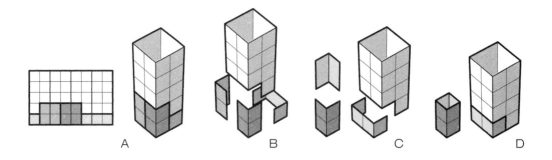

THE CHALLENGING BLOCK

Using a universal set of three rectangular building blocks, 1 X 1 X 2, 1 X 2 X 3, and 1 X 2 X 4, as shown in illustration A, you can cover any area within your 4 X 4 town block from 1 single square, 1 X 1 up, to 16 squares, as shown in illustrations 1 through 16, respectively.

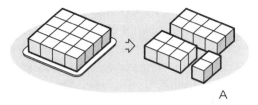

A

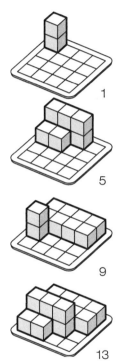 1

2

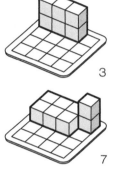 3

4

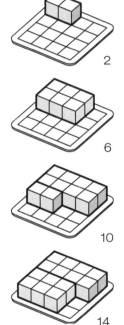 5

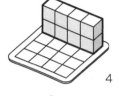 6

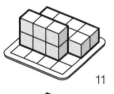 7

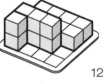 8

9

10

11

12

13

14

15

16

A half-cube flat color brick can be inverted into another rectangular brick with a fully uncolored surface in two steps. First, cut the colored brick into three triangular prisms and reassemble them as shown in diagram A into the new brick shown in diagram B. Second, make a horizontal cut and put the top half of the new brick under the bottom one as shown in diagram B. You will get the fully uncolored brick shown in diagram C.

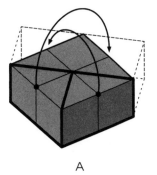
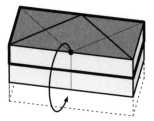
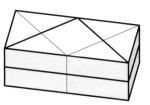

A   B   C

A regular solid tetrahedron (A) consists of four equal trilateral pyramids, each of which has as its base one of the tetrahedron's faces, and its vertex coincides with the central point of the tetrahedron; this point is marked with a black dot. First, divide the tetrahedron into two equal pieces as shown in diagram B. Each consists of two equal trilateral pyramids. Then, divide one of these pieces into two separate pyramids as shown in diagram C. Now we have three pieces—one double piece and two single ones. Rearrange the two single pyramids around the double piece as shown in diagram D. After that, place all three pieces together so that the single pyramids cover with their bases (dark faces) the two dark faces on the double one. You will get a new solid (E), with its surface fully uncolored.

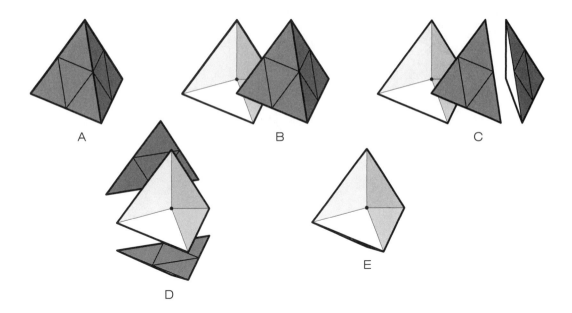

A

B

C

D

E

CUBICAL INVERSION

To invert a dark cube into a light one, follow the six steps shown below.

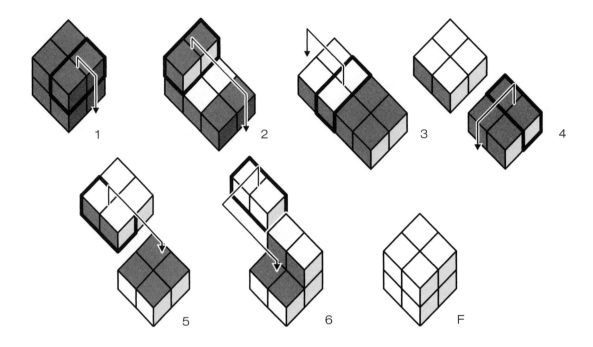

THE MATCHSTICK SNAKE ON A CUBE

The degree-30 matchstick snake-15 (its graph) on the surface of a unit cube is shown in diagrams A (on the cube layout) and B. In the graph, the lighter lines represent matchsticks on the front faces of the cube (as they are oriented in diagram B), darker ones, on its back faces.

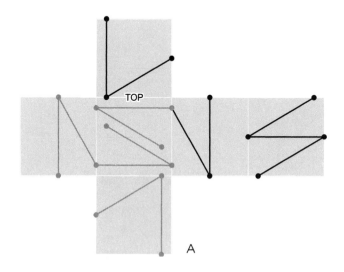

A

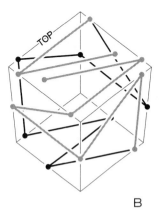

B

INDEX

Note: Page references in *italics* refer to solutions.

All the King's Men, 207, *326*

Ancient Butterfly, 201, *323*

Arrow-Head Connection, 56–57, *256*

Bees & Ladybugs, 189–190, *315*

Bermuda Pearls, 105, 272

Big Bee Challenge, 191, *316*

Billiard Ball Trap Challenge, 60–61, *257*

Bouquet of Bulbs, 52, *255*

Buttons, Needles & Threads, 53–54, *256*

Cat & Chair, 74, *261*

Challenge of Cat Cradle, 202, *323*

Challenge of the Green Line, 69, *260*

Challenge of the Pyramid, 19, *245*

Challenge of the Wall Maze, 138–139, *290*

Challenging Block, 236, *341*

Challenging Diamond, 27, *247*

Challenging Hopscotch, 194, *318*

Challenging mix, 210–240, *244. See also specific puzzles*

Change Coin Rows, 94, *269*

Change the Columns, 186–187, *313*

Change the Levels, 184, *311*

Change the Rooks, 209, *328*

Checkered Dominoes, 113–114, *274*

Checkered Mountain, 177, *308*

Checkered Multiplication, 31, *248*

Checkered Origami Trimino, 163, *301*

Checkered Q, 28, *247*

Checkered Rectangles, 102, *271*

Checkered Tangram: Dog, Fox, Goose & Corn, 116–117, *275*

Checkered Trimino, 171, *305*

Christmas-Tree & Square, 39, *251*

Coin puzzles, 73, *242. See also specific puzzles*

Color Candy Chain, 68, *259*

Color Comb Zigzag, 70, *260*

Color Grains Puzzle, 119, *276*

Cone Challenge, 230, *337*

Constellation of the Crescent, 48, *254*

Cottage, 82, *263*

Counters, 182–183

Cracker Dissection, 21, *245*

Cross the Lake, 208, *327*

Cubical Inversion, 239, *344*

Diagonal Crisscross, 180, *310*

Dicey Connections, 51, *255*

Dissection puzzles, 16–41, *241. See also specific puzzles*

Distorted Pentashapes, 110, *274*

Divide the Grid, 22, *246*

Dot-connections, 42–71, *241–242. See also specific puzzles*

Double Unicursal Grid, 63, *258*

Dragon Circuit, 64, *258*

Dragon Squaring, 36, *250*

Drumming Moves, 200, *322*

Eight Counters in Octagon, 197, *319*

Eight-Into-Zero Change, 149, *294*

Eight Stick Challenge, 214, *330*

Fenced Knight's Tour, 223–224, *334*
Fence Puzzle, 215, *330*
Field of Hearts Challenge, 126, *281*
Fishbone Puzzle, 203, *324*
Five Y's, 212, *329*
Flower Arrow, 44, *253*
Flying Bird, 77, *262*
Fold Two to Three, 156, *297*
Four Arrows, 101, *271*
Four Coin Squares, 97, *270*
4 – 3 =, 144, *292*
Foxy Box, 134, *288*
Framed Move Challenge, 193, *317*

Grid-and-piece puzzles, 98–99. *See also specific puzzles*
Grid Changes, 40, *252*

Hard as XYZ, 140–141, *291*
Hexa-Flower, 93, *269*
Hexagonal Crisscross, 192, *317*
Hexa Six, 147, *293*
Hexa-Spiral Path Puzzle, 120, *276*
Hexa Three-by-Three, 108, *273*
Hexa X-Changes, 198, *320*
Hide the Color, 238, *343*
Holes in a Checkerboard, 30, *248*
How Many Candies?, 124, *280*

If & Then, 142, *291*
Interlocked Rings, 121–122, *277*
In the Domino Mood, 50, *255*

Invert a Color Brick, 237, *342*
Invisible Digital Tiling, 151, *295*

Join Eight Marbles, 45, *253*

Knight Maze, 204, *325*
Knight-rook Exchange, 206, *326*
Knight's Maneuvers, 205, *325*
Knight's Tetra-Connections, 58–59, *257*

Lake & Mountain, 178, *309*
Letter Quest, 132, *286–287*
Letter Weeding, 131, *285*
Lines-Through-Dots, 71, *260*
Little Origami Chessboard, 179, *309*

Magic 3 × 3 Dissection, 148, *293*
Manta's Puzzle, 25, *246*
Marquee, 84, *264*
Match Connections, 55, *256*
Match Similarity, 79, *262*
Matchstick puzzles, 72–73, *242. See also specific puzzles*
Matchstick Snake in a Circle, 219, *333*
Matchstick Snake on a Cube, 240, *345*
Matchstick snake puzzles, 210–211, *244. See also specific puzzles*

Mice & Cat, 135, *289*
Molecular Chain Puzzle, 107, *273*
Molecular Dissection, 35, *250*
Moon & Star, 137, *290*
Mountain Seasons, 176, *308*
Moves in the H, 185, *312*

Nautilus Puzzle, 18, *245*
Neo Matchstick Snake, 216, *331*
Nine Bat-Squares, 111, *274*
Not One Rhombus, 76, *261*

One Square, 136, *289*
O-O-O-O Puzzle, 129, *283*
Origami Checkerboard Puzzle, 165–166, *302–303*
Origami Domino, 170, *305*
Origami Greek Cross, 169, *304*
Origami Hill, 174, *307*
Origami House Puzzle, 168, *304*
Origami Mini-Dominoes, 158–159, *298*
Origami Propeller, 167, *303*
Origami puzzles, 154–181, *242–243. See also specific puzzles*
Origami Window, 181, *310*

Paper Cube Puzzle, 233, *339*
Paper Tetrahedron Puzzle, 234, *340*

Pattern puzzles, 98–126, *242. See also specific puzzles*
Pectoral Puzzle, 37, *251*
Penta-Coin Change, 88, *266*
Place & Turn, 220–221, *333*
Plate Packing (4K-5I), 231–232, *338*
Polygons for the Matchstick Snake, 217–218, *332*
PUZZLE Connection, 49, *254*
Puzzle Constellation, 47, *254*
Puzzle of the "VII," 145, *292*
Puzzle Park, 115, *275*
Puzzler's Merry-Go-Round, 143, *291*

Q-Grid Puzzle, 23, *246*
Quadragonal, 86, *265*
Quadrangles, 123, *278–279*
Quick Puzzle, 133, *288*

Racetrack Puzzle, 67, *259*
Redirect the Corner, 87, *265*
Red Triangle Puzzle, 225, *335*
Reed Number Maze, 153, *296*
Restore the Button, 34, *250*

Seven Depots Puzzle, 65, *258*
Shark Challenge, 24, *246*
Shield Challenge, 32, *249*
Shoe, 83, *264*

Six Wire Corners, 213, *329*

Skew Domino Pattern, 173, *306*

Skew Rectangle, 80, *263*

Skew Trimino Pattern, 164, *301*

Slide the Row, 91, *267*

Softy Challenge, 227–228, *336*

Spinning Puzzle, 196, *319*

Spiral Galaxy Mystery, 188, *314*

Square & Division, 81, *263*

Squared Color Spots, 104, *272*

Squared Eight, 41, *252*

Square Rearrangement, 199, *321*

Squares in the Window, 75, *261*

Squaring the Arrow, 38, *251*

Star & Cross, 29, *247*

Star of Origami, 162, *301*

Stars & Spirals, 46, *253*

Tangrammed Checkerboard, 103, *271*

T-Coin Challenge, 92, *268*

Test-Fest, 128, *282*

Tetra-Marbles, 106, *272*

Three-Into-One Folds, 157, *297*

Three-Strip-Triangle, 160, *298*

Time Pictoscope, 125, *281*

Touch-Me-Not Blocks, 112, *274*

Triads, 95, *270*

Triangle Addition, 33, *249*

Triangle-In-Rectangle, 172, *306*

Triangle Table Puzzle, 26, *246*

Tricky moves, 182–209, *244. See also specific puzzles*

Tri-Hex Puzzle, 109, *273*

Triple Cut, 20, *245*

Trisection of Octagon, 85, *264*

Turn Up the Shell, 89, *266*

Twelve Rows of Coins, 96, *270*

Twin-move puzzles, 182–183. *See also specific puzzles*

Twisting Paper Snake, 66, *259*

Two Joined Squares, 195, *318*

Two Matching Areas, 78, *262*

Two Sides of the Mountain, 175, *307*

Two Similar Tubes, 235, *340*

Two Weaving Loops, 222, *334*

Unicursal Tangram Bird, 62, *257*

Vertical Flip-Flop, 90, *267*

Visual patterns, 99

Waffle Puzzle, 100, *271*

Wire Count, 152, *295*

Wooden Patterns Puzzle, 229, *336*

Words & numbers, 127–153, 242. *See also specific puzzles*

Word Tower, 130, *284*

Woven Colored Square, 161, *299–300*

Wrap the Box, 118, *276*

X-Symmetry Challenge, 146, *292*

Yellow Cube Puzzle, 226, *335*

Zero-Infinity Mystery, 150, *294*

ABOUT THE AUTHOR

Serhiy Grabarchuk is a metagrobologist—one whose life interest is puzzles and puzzling. He started his puzzling activities thirty-nine years ago when he was eight. Since then, Serhiy has been active in many different aspects of puzzling. He continuously invents and creates new, never-seen-before puzzles, makes puzzle prototypes and has his puzzle designs produced, collects original puzzles and solves hundreds of them every year, researches puzzles and their multifaceted history, compiles and publishes original books, participates in major international puzzle events and gatherings, and seeks to encourage young gifted puzzle persons.

Serhiy has created several thousand puzzles of varying types, which often invoke new puzzle principles and have original mathematical, physical, and visual ideas behind them. His puzzle designs were (and still are) produced by many puzzle companies all around the world, such as Haba, Bits & Pieces, and Binary Arts (now, ThinkFun), and others. His puzzles have been published in different books and periodicals including *Games* magazine, *Quark* magazine, *Pa-Zu-Ru*, *CFF*, *Quantum* magazine, *Charade*, *Field of Wonders*, *Archimedes*, and many others. Serhiy's puzzles can also be seen and played on numerous puzzle Web sites, and many of his puzzles are used as part of different puzzle contests—virtual (on the Web) and real (in various puzzle events).

Serhiy worked on numerous puzzle projects and continues to collaborate with many prominent puzzle folks, such as Nob Yoshigahara, Jerry Slocum, Will Shortz, Sjaak Griffioen, Bill Ritchie, Steve Wagner, Alan Segal, Nancy Alliegro, Rodolfo Kurchan, Nevzat Erkmen, Bob Kirkland, Anatoly Kalinin, Harry Nelson, Nick Baxter, Ed Pegg Jr., Kate Jones, Scott Kim, John Conway, Andy Liu, Oskar van Deventer, Wei-Hwa Huang, Andrea Gilbert, Shelly Hazard, Gianni Sarcone, Marie-Jo Waeber, as well as other great puzzle designers, mathematicians, and magicians from all over the world.

Serhiy owns a large collection of puzzles and games, and maintains a comprehensive puzzle library. He has compiled and published about a dozen collections of his original puzzles. Serhiy likes to make puzzles by himself, and for many years manufactured hundreds of different wooden, plastic, metal, and paper puzzles in his home workshop.

Serhiy was educated as an engineer in fine mechanics. He has five puzzle patents. Serhiy has won several prestigious international puzzle design competitions; among them is the Hikimi Wooden Puzzle Competition. Serhiy's passion for graphic arts in small forms has allowed him, during his puzzle life to make thousands of drawings of puzzle designs, a comprehensive puzzle and game card index, catalogs and books, and several dozen trademarks. For more than two years, Serhiy ran the Web site www.puzzles.com.

Serhiy is a skilled puzzle solver and has taken part in the World Puzzle Championships several times, as a participant or team captain. Serhiy now is the vice president of the Ukrainian Federation of Puzzlesport, and the captain of the Ukrainian Puzzle Team, and he represents Ukraine's puzzle interests in the World Puzzle Federation.

From a very young age Serhiy has enjoyed magic. There is a well-known connection between magic and puzzling, as exemplified in the work of Martin Gardner, Nob Yoshigahara, and Mark Setteducati. Martin Gardner has in many ways served as a teacher and mentor to Serhiy.

Serhiy's nonpuzzling interests cover modern and classical music, including jazz and blues; photography and cinematography; musicals; and puppet shows. Serhiy and his wife Tanya have two sons, Serhiy Jr. (twenty-five) and Peter (nineteen). He lives with his family in a small town in the western part of Ukraine, where Serhiy's family very actively helps and supports him in his puzzling endeavors.

WHAT IS MENSA?

Mensa
The High IQ Society

Mensa is the international society for people with a high IQ. We have more than 100,000 members in over 40 countries worldwide.

The society's aims are:
• to identify and foster human intelligence for the benefit of humanity;
• to encourage research in the nature, characteristics, and uses of intelligence;
• to provide a stimulating intellectual and social environment for its members.

Anyone with an IQ score in the top two percent of the population is eligible to become a member of Mensa—are you the "one in 50" we've been looking for?

Mensa membership offers an excellent range of benefits:
• Networking and social activities nationally and around the world;
• Special Interest Groups (hundreds of chances to pursue your hobbies and interests—from art to zoology!);
• Monthly International Journal, national magazines, and regional newsletters;
• Local meetings—from game challenges to food and drink;
• National and international weekend gatherings and conferences;
• Intellectually stimulating lectures and seminars;
• Access to the worldwide SIGHT network for travelers and hosts.

For more information about Mensa International:
www.mensa.org
Mensa International
15 The Ivories
6–8 Northampton Street
Islington, London N1 2HY
United Kingdom

For more information about American Mensa:
www.us.mensa.org
Telephone: (800) 66-MENSA
American Mensa Ltd.
1229 Corporate Drive West
Arlington, TX 76006-6103 USA

For more information about British Mensa (UK and Ireland):
www.mensa.org.uk
Telephone: +44 (0) 1902 772771
E-mail: enquiries@mensa.org.uk
British Mensa Ltd.
St. John's House
St. John's Square
Wolverhampton WV2 4AH
United Kingdom

What Is Mensa?